Tips & Traps
for Growing and Maintaining
the Perfect Lawn

Tips & Traps
for Growing and Maintaining
the Perfect Lawn

Rodney Johns

McGRAW-HILL

New York   Chicago   San Francisco   Lisbon   London
Madrid   Mexico City   Milan   New Delhi   San Juan
Seoul   Singapore   Sydney   Toronto

Copyright © 2006 by The McGraw-Hill Companies, Inc. All rights reserved.
Printed in the United States of America. Except as permitted under the
United States Copyright Act of 1976, no part of this publication may be
reproduced or distributed in any form or by any means, or stored in a data
base or retrieval system, without the prior written permission of the pub-
lisher.

1 2 3 4 5 6 7 8 9 0   DOC/DOC   0 1 2 1 0 9 8 7 6

ISBN 0-07-146860-9

The sponsoring editor for this book was Cary Sullivan and the production
supervisor was Pamela A. Pelton. It was set in Garamond by Lone Wolf
Enterprises, Ltd. The art director for the cover was Handel Low.

Printed and bound by RR Donnelley.

McGraw-Hill books are available at special quantity discounts to use as
premiums and sales promotions, or for use in corporate training programs.
For more information, please write to the Director of Special Sales,
McGraw-Hill Professional, Two Penn Plaza, New York, NY 10121-2298.
Or contact your local bookstore.

 This book is printed on recycled, acid-free paper containing a
minimum of 50% recycled, de-inked fiber.

I dedicate this book to my daughter Taylor Johns.

This book is such a small accomplishment compared to the joy you have brought into my life. May you always be true to the ones you love. Never lie to anyone, and remember your actions, no matter how big or small, will always be *your* actions.

I will always be proud of you.

Love, Dad

Contents

About the Author

 Rodney Johns served in the golf course industry for nearly 10 years. He currently operates Arki-Tec Landscaping and Sales LLC in Canton, MO. Arki-Tec was started in 1995 and has grown to be a large lawn and garden center which also sells various types of equipment. www.arki-tec.com has become one of the world's most popular websites for lawn and garden equipment. Rodney serves on various academic advisory boards and is a huge promoter of education in the field of horticulture. He has written other books on turfgrass management and co-authored books on pesticide application. He has various degrees in plant science, and turf and greenhouse management.

Foreword

The writing of this book was a major undertaking. It was a life-long dream to author a text, but I had no idea of the number of hours involved and the sacrifices that many others had to endure to make this happen.

Several people assisted me with this endeavor and I wish to thank them for their encouragement, support, and patience. You all know who you are and, at the risk of leaving a name out, I am not going to list everyone. I hope you understand.

To my students, former and current, thank you all. I want each of you to know that I learned from you as well and there was rarely a class that went by that I didn't pick something up from you.

There is, however, one person that without her help this would not have been possible. Her understanding and love has been an inspiration to me. My wife, Heather, has been my sounding board, loudest critic, and biggest supporter. She always has some words of wisdom for me and has sacrificed more than I have during this process. For all of these things, I want to thank her from the bottom of my heart. Honey, you're the best! Without you, I could not have completed this task.

Planning for the Greenest Grass

INTRODUCTION

The process of creating the perfect lawn is not something that can happen overnight nor is it something that can happen with little effort. It not only takes time to get the perfect lawn established, but it also takes time to keep the perfect lawn in good condition. Whether you are the kind of person that likes to do your own lawn work or prefers to hire a lawn care company to do your work, I will help you achieve the perfect lawn and keep it looking that way. Lawns prevent erosion, reduce pollution, provide outdoor recreational areas, and help break up the concrete suburbia we continue to create.

Lawn care and landscaping have always been considered to be subjective when it comes to what people want. One person's idea of a perfect lawn may be a little different than what someone else thinks to be "good enough." To me, the idea of the perfect lawn is one that is weed-free with a dark green color, tolerant to periods of dry weather, and overall is just very appealing to the eye. I think that anyone is capable of having a decent-looking lawn but to achieve the perfect lawn, strategies must be put into place and the lawn must be cared for during the entire calendar year.

Here are some key questions for starting over with your lawn:

- Do I have more weeds than I do grass?
- If I pulled up to my house in a car would I be impressed by what I saw?
- Do I have a large number of weeds in the yard that are visible from a distance?
- Does my neighbor's yard look better than mine?
- When is the last time I used a fertilizer or weed killer on the lawn?
- Have I applied lime to my yard in the last three years?
- Is my yard bumpy or uneven?
- Does water stand in my yard?
- Are there places in the lawn where grass will not grow at all?

All of these questions will help you to understand if your project is one of starting over or if you can do something to your existing lawn to make it better. Starting with question number one, "Do I have more weeds in my lawn than grass?" As a rule of thumb, if your lawn contains more than 50 percent weeds at any point, you are probably at a start-over point. It is very difficult to get a lawn back under control if all you have are weeds in the yard to begin with. However, removal of those weeds can leave you with a very sparse and barren lawn.

Ideally we are all after the same result, which is to have a yard that really has some curb side appeal. It would be nice if, when someone pulled up to your home, they saw the lawn as a really attractive feature. It is a proven fact that if you have a well-landscaped home with a good-looking manicured yard, you can potentially add value to the home; and resell the home for more money should you choose to put your house on the market. Lawns are a key part to the overall landscape. Lawns accent homes and create enjoyable outdoor areas for a variety of reasons.

DID YOU KNOW?
Getting a few weeds under control can easily be done while promoting the growth of your healthy grass at the same time.

PRO POINTER
Strong curb appeal sells houses and raises home values.

FIGURE 1-1
Weed-infested yard—starting over would make the most sense.

TECH TIP
Lawns are a key element in the overall land-scape.

Lawns tend to vary slightly in condition from one community to the next. Your lawn-care program, unfortunately, may be only as good as your neighbor's lawn-care program. Having the perfect lawn is an ongoing challenge just to compete with Mother Nature's fury. When you add a neighbor into the mix of things, the lawn and the challenge becomes much more difficult.

Many weeds are prolific seeders and they can spread out and produce thousands of seed heads in a very short period of time. Lawns that lie nestled in communities where everyone treats their lawns properly are much easier to keep looking good from year to year because there is less chance of encroachment from your neighbor's weed problem.

TECH TIP
If your neighbor has a lawn that is full of weeds and you are constantly spraying your yard but never seem to get ahead, it may be a result of your neighbor's lack of lawn care instead of whatever it is you think you are doing wrong.

The next big key to having a great lawn is not to forget your lawn after getting a great start. Lawn care is exactly that, "care for the lawn." This means that there are things you should be doing all year to keep a lawn looking its best.

BEATING WEEDS

Weed control is one of the most important factors that go along with that. If you do not control weeds on a year to year basis you will have weeds that will come back in and take over your yard. You should have a preventative schedule in place to not only control existing weeds but also a schedule that will keep new weeds from coming into the lawn. It is important to keep up that schedule and repeat the treatments on a year to year basis. Do not think you can skip a year: In that time you could potentially have thousands of new weeds take over your yard. Spend the money each year to make sure that the lawn stays looking its best.

FIGURE 1-2
Pictured is a good lawn next to a weed-infested lawn. No matter how good your lawn treatment program is, neighbors can be a source of new weeds into your lawn.

I hear so often that, "I put fertilizers on my yard and nothing happens. Why would I need to put lime on my yard?

> **PRO POINTER**
> Lime is one of the cheapest and easiest ways to solve many problems in many yards.

What good will a soil test do?" Lime is one of the cheapest and easiest ways to solve problems in many yards. I will say over and over again that lime is a cure overlooked by many in the industry. When is the last time the person who treated your lawn asked you about doing a soil test or potentially adding lime to the yard? A soil test in most areas can be done through a local extension office or sometimes even through a cooperative. A soil test for a basic analysis is less than $20 and that test can tell you more answers to your problems then you can imagine. A soil test should be one of the first things to consider when even thinking of correcting lawn care problems. It will tell you what you need to know about soil ph and soil fertility. I will get more into the details of lime and soil testing later on but these are things to consider in the early stages. Following is a list of obstacles:

- An obvious decision maker for when to start over with a lawn is when it is uneven and out of sorts.
- Slightly rough yards do not mean that it is time to start over necessarily. Earthworm activity can make the top of the ground seem bumpier than normal.
- Grading issues, where water runs towards the house, instead of away from it, is a problem you have to deal with.
- Situations where water pools in parts of a yard need attention.

Any of these scenarios could be a reason to start over. Look at seeding or sodding your lawn from scratch, that way grade issues can be corrected and lawns can be established on even ground.

It seems many lawns have areas that will not grow grass but there are several potential causes for bare spots in the lawn. Here is a list of issues that may help you to troubleshoot why you might have a few bare spots around the lawn:

- Not having enough light penetration through trees to grow grass can create bare spots
- Dog urine starts bare spots
- Very low soil ph causes bare spots
- A need for fertilizer is noticed when bare spots appear
- Chemical or fuel spills can cause bare spots
- Water standing in a lawn for long periods of time will make bare spots

- Damage from mowers, people, or machinery may make bare spots

- Drought or dry periods, without proper irrigation, are a source of bare spots

I will tell you ways to eliminate bare spots later on but these issues should all be considered when you are planning for a major lawn renovation. This is especially true when looking at a bare spot that may have been caused by chemicals.

> **PRO POINTER**
> Chemical spills could be a situation where you may have an area of contaminated soil that would need to be removed and replaced with new soil in order to eliminate the bare spot. I have seen fertilizer or even gas spills that will persist in the lawn for literally a few years.

WORKING WITH THE LAWN YOU ALREADY HAVE

As I said, everyone has a reason for starting over with their lawn. You now know several reasons for making the decision to start over with your lawn project. There may be other reasons that you are thinking about for not starting over with the lawn project, and trying to work with what grass you already have. What if you are still unsure if starting over is the right choice, and you want to try and salvage the lawn that is already there? There is still hope for you also. When can you work with the turfgrass you already have? Following are the answers:

- The lawn has few weeds and there is a lot of "good" grass in the yard.

- There are a few bare spots, but overall the yard is healthy.

- The lawn has a decent color and you fertilize it each year.

- You try to kill weeds but never seem to get rid of all of them.

- You are willing to take the time not to have to mess with the mud and hassle of reseeding.

- If it will be very costly to start a lawn over from seed or sod and you do not have the money to do such a project.

These are a few reasons for working with your existing yard and not starting over from scratch and I am sure you may have some additional reasoning when thinking about your own yard.

There is one huge factor to consider when and if you decide that you are going to work with the existing grass you already have. You have to make an evaluation to either control the weeds you have or to get some better, thicker grass to grow in the yard. It is nearly impossible to do both at the same time of the year. The biggest determining factor for that might be the time of the year in which you are making your decision to improve your lawn.

TECH TIP
The fall is by far the best time of the year to try to establish new turfgrass in any lawn. Fall can also be a great time to control broadleaf weeds so this can create a dilemma over which to do first.

Lawns that contain high numbers of weeds can often choke out the good grass before it gets time to really take hold and get established. This creates a situation where it is almost critical to control the weeds you have before even considering starting over with any type of seeding or establishment procedure. If it is the late fall and you are establishing new grass, the new grass will be vigorous enough to compete with any weeds you have in the lawn, in most cases. However you must have plans to control weeds first thing in the spring or your efforts might have been wasted.

Here is one point I will bring up later on and it is another good rule of thumb when considering weed control vs. seeding time. You need at least six weeks or two mowings between the time of any type of seeding and a chemical treatment.

When you are working with your existing grass the best way to improve your turf is by using a method to inner seed your existing grass that is already there. There are many methods to getting new grass to grow but again the timing is the most critical part.

PRO POINTER
New weeds will start growing very early in the spring and you must start to control them as soon as you possibly can.

PLANNING FOR YOUR LAWN

Planning for a lawn project requires something to be done in most months of the year. This includes months in which lawn care is the last thing on some people's minds. Many of the common mistakes made in lawn care have to do with the timing of fertilizer and weed control treatments. Here are just a couple of examples of the overall thought process it takes to keep a beautiful looking lawn throughout the year. It is a strategy program for starting over with a new lawn in cool season turf:

> **DID YOU KNOW?**
> Young seedling grass can often be affected by chemicals so it is critical that there be sufficient time for your grass seedlings to establish themselves. I will cover more on other chemical effects and seeding issues later on.

- August—Spray all of your existing turf with Roundup® to kill all vegetation, which includes all of your existing grass and any possible evasive weeds.

- September—This is the time to do your seeding or sodding project. Make sure you do not take shortcuts because this will just cause more problems later on.

- October/November—Make sure you have adequate fertilizer to keep your grass growing strong through the winter.

- February/March—Start a good weed control program that you will be prepared to stick with throughout the year. The first round will be a pre-emergent herbicide that will prevent weeds, later on, in the growing season.

- April/May—Now is when you need to reflect on all of the "junk" that took over your yard and that you got rid of by starting over with a lawn. Keep things going with a broadleaf application to get rid of those pesky weeds before they take hold again.

- May/June—Do not forget about grub worms. Now is the time to get a treatment down to keep grubs under control from year to year.

- June/August—It will not hurt to use small doses of fertilizer in a liquid form, but really your yard has no major needs for fertilizer until fall if you have cool season grasses.

- September–November—You should be enjoying a lavish lawn that has been weed free and cared for all summer. Make sure you give it that last good blast of fertilizer to carry it through the winter.

Here is a strategy program for one year working with your existing lawn and trying to improve the grass you have in cool season turf:

- January/February—Get a weed control program laid out for the year. Figure out which chemicals you are going to use if you are doing it yourself, or start talking to lawn care companies if you are looking to hire someone.

- February/March—Be prepared to start putting chemicals on the yard to control weeds early. Many weeds that do not show up until June or July need to be controlled now. Crabgrass is an example of one of those weeds that once you have seen it, it might be too late.

- March/April—Now is when broadleaf weeds are really getting started well. You will want to try to get these under control if you are thinking about doing any seeding in the fall. Make sure that you have eliminated as many weeds as possible so that the new grass will have a better chance for survival.

- May/June—It's time to think about grubs if you have them. Also it is probably time for a second round of a pre-emergent. This is your last your chance to get those broadleaf weeds before summer also.

- June/August—Time to coast a little. Mid summer fertilizer is never a good idea in high amounts unless you are using small amounts of a liquid fertilizer.

- August/September—Now is the best time to seed for the whole year. Plan for a seeding program that will use aeration, slit seeding, or power raking to incorporate the seed into the soil.

- September/November—Now that your seed is growing, do not forget that a winter fertilizer will be needed to keep things going.

Lawns that follow a year around program are much more resilient and hold up better against drought conditions. Nothing is set in stone and your particular target date can vary slightly by geographic location. People in Southern states need to start much earlier than the people in the Northern states when looking at previous examples.

Lawns are composed of plants, and are living things with complex cell structures. Plants respond to environmental conditions and we all learn new things about lawn care every day. You need to think about hiring a professional when it comes to wanting that really meticulous lawn.

> **PRO POINTER**
> Ask the right questions to insure the person you are hiring knows what they are talking about. As methods change and more is discovered about improving lawn care, strategies improve for handling lawn problems. There is a lot more to having and maintaining a good lawn than most people realize. Try to hire someone who knows more than just how to mow a lawn.

Here is a checklist of questions you should ask when hiring a lawn care professional:

- How many lawns have you installed and where are they located?

- What are the names of those people and can I call them for a reference?

- Do you do lawn applications, and can you continue to take care of my lawn throughout the year should I choose to hire you?

- Do you have the licenses necessary to legally and safely apply chemicals to my yard?

- Do you charge to give estimates about my lawn, and what I need to do?

- How many years experience do you have in the lawn care business or turf industry?

The answers to these questions will quickly help you decide if the person you are talking to is really the right person for the job.

OPTIONS AVAILABLE TO CORRECT YOUR LAWN PROBLEMS

I can safely say that once an evaluation of the lawn is made, you are faced with the decision of what to do with your lawn problems. Let's start with the basics and work our way up. I will get into very detailed sections about each one of these topics later on, but is important to be thinking about the possible solutions as you evaluate the problems.

Too many times I have seen my own customers rely on a short period of weed control thinking that the yard will just kind of start to take care of itself at some point. For instance, I have dealt with customers that will spend thousands of dollars to renovate a yard, only to let weeds come in and take over only one year after the yard has been renovated. Weed control is simply the easiest thing to do on a year to year basis to eliminate long term problems later on.

Aeration is a process that creates air exchange with the atmosphere, reduces compaction, and creates a good seed bed for new grass. If weeds have "choked" out the good grass in the lawn then this process may help to rejuvenate the lawn you already have. Weed control will still need to be done at some point to allow the "good grasses" to compete, but aeration can help to eliminate many problems. Weeds may have been the source of the problem to begin with, but as weeds tend to take over the lawn the desirable grass becomes in worse condition. It is a combination of good lawn care practices such as aeration along with a yearly weed control program that help to make the difference.

Power raking a yard can improve turf quality. A power rake is a device the shreds thatch while creating a seed bed for new turfgrass as you go. This process costs about the same and takes about the same amount of time as the aeration process. Again the goal is to help

TECH TIP
Weed control is simply the easiest thing to do on a year to year basis to eliminate long term problems later on.

the new grass to compete by creating a seed bed and providing an environment conducive to growing grass. There will need to be time taken to remove the thatch that is pulled up by this process.

You have a couple of options for establishing cool season grasses. One option is a seeding project that literally would be completely starting over from bare soil. Now seeding in this manner allows you to correct drainage issues, bury old weeds and debris, incorporate fertilizers, while creating a new seed bed at the same time. There are many benefits to being able to directly improve the soil. Also seeding is much cheaper than sodding.

FIGURE 1-3
Using a power rake or an aerator.

DID YOU KNOW?
Sod is one of the most expensive processes that exists when creating a new lawn or renovating an old one.

Another option is to use a sodding process which can be done in a couple of different fashions. In most cases, the soil is turned over and rolled out with a roller and new sod is installed over the soil like a carpet. The other way is to cover the existing soil with sod without turning over the soil. In any instance, sod usage must be done correctly to have long term success with this type of process. Although your grass may look really good when it is first rolled out, sod is not as easy of a fix as most think it is.

2

Climate Considerations and Turf Types

Turfgrass species vary in the areas that they grow in for a variety of reasons. There is a specific type of turf that will thrive in a location or, be at least, suitable to grow under a range of conditions. To be successful in establishing turfgrass you need to have a basic understanding of the types of grasses and the locations suitable for each variety of turf to be planted in. These locations are called hardiness zones.

HARDINESS ZONES—TURF TYPES

The first thing that should be considered when selecting a turf type is the zonal requirements or more specifically the difference in warm season and cool season grasses. The warm season grasses for the most part are considered to grow in the bottom half of the United States, or other warm climates and are not susceptible to long periods of freezing temperatures. Some of the grass types are not capable of handling frost or freezing temperatures for even one night. Other warm season grasses can handle cold temperatures but perhaps not below 0 temperatures.

The basic types of warm season grasses that will grow in these regions are:

- Bermuda grass
- Zoysia grass
- Carpet grass
- St. Augustine grass
- Centipede grass

The cool season grasses are just the opposite in where they are most acclimated to survival. Cool season grasses are usually found in climates in the Northern half of the United States and other climates which are cooler and more moderate in temperature conditions. Grasses in these areas usually prefer moderate to heavy rainfall and do not like hot, dry, or arid conditions that would typically be found in the south.

The cool season types of grasses used in these climate locations are:

- Bluegrass
- Fescues

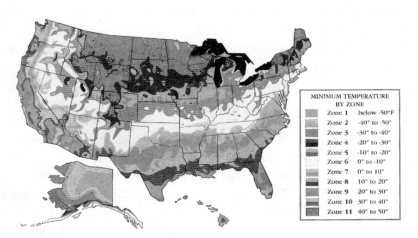

MINIMUM TEMPERATURE
BY ZONE

Zone 1	below -50°F
Zone 2	-40° to -50°
Zone 3	-30° to -40°
Zone 4	-20° to -30°
Zone 5	-10° to -20°
Zone 6	0° to -10°
Zone 7	0° to 10°
Zone 8	10° to 20°
Zone 9	20° to 30°
Zone 10	30° to 40°
Zone 11	40° to 50°

FIGURE 2-1
USDA Zonal Map—This map can help you determine what grass will grow best in your region.

- Ryegrass

- Bentgrass

There is however a large section of the United States that is both hot and cold during the calendar year.

> **PRO POINTER**
>
> In the transition zone, the problem is that winters can be too cold for one type of grass and too warm for another.

This region is referred to as the Transition Zone and is a sweeping area that extends right through the middle of the United States. The transition zone often has the problem of winters being too cold for one type of grass and too warm for another type of grass. This zone encompasses a large area through the Midwest due to the unpredictable weather that exists in that region. In many cases there are warm season grasses planted in the same neighborhoods with cool season grasses all in the same block. Growing conditions can leave either turf type in poor condition during given times of the year.

Rainfall is very critical to growing grass; the reason being is plants are mostly composed of water. When grass does not have adequate moisture turfgrass establishment is very difficult. When you are thinking about growing grass you should also take a look at soil type,

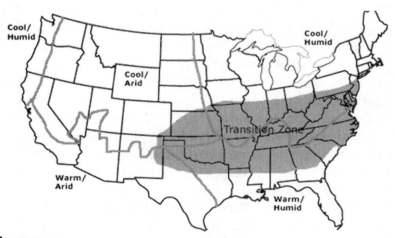

FIGURE 2-2
Regions for turfgrass—Warm season, cool season, and transition zones.

temperature, exposure, light, traffic, and most importantly the specific function of the grass you are planting.

COOL SEASON GRASSES AND NORTHERN CLIMATES

Most of the grasses planted in the U.S. still fall under the category of cool season grasses. Some of these grasses are adapted to warmer climates, and the transition zone, but for the most part cool season grasses prefer exactly what they are called, cool seasons. There is a need for high fertility and a luxurious amount of water for most types. If you live in the northern reaches of the United States these types of grasses will be a must and any one that is the South would virtually not be able to use most of these turf types at all. Understanding what type of grass you have and potentially what type of grass you might need is step one of the planning process.

TECH TIP

The first step of the planning process is understanding what type of grass you have and what type of grass you might need.

Kentucky Bluegrass

The most common cool season grass which is grown widely in the North and also in a large part of the Transition Zone is Kentucky blue grass or Poa pratensis. Kentucky bluegrass is the thin bladed plant that is used in lawns, golf courses, and many other recreational facilities. It can spread vegetative by tillers and rhizomes. It is a fairly aggressive spreader and can repair itself when damaged from shoes, tires, or golf clubs. It can thrive under rigorous mowing conditions and is commonly maintained at a height of anywhere from 1 ½" to over a height of 3" or more. Bluegrass can be grown for use in a lawn or can even be used on golf tees. The grass has a very good color and when fertilized makes a very attractive area of turf.

Bluegrass was introduced into the U.S. in the 1700's and is believed to originate in Middle Eastern Europe. It was first used here in the United States in Jamestown. It has been planted in lawns for many years and adapts to a range of growing conditions. The earlier

FIGURE 2-3
Dry Bluegrass turf—Although this bluegrass looks dead, once
the rains start again this lawn can quickly recover.

varieties were considered to be somewhat troubled by disease problems and required high rates of seed to establish. With newer varieties being more suitable for warm weather, and less susceptible to disease, the choices and conditions for growing Kentucky bluegrass continue to improve.

Kentucky bluegrass is best suited for full sun to lightly shaded areas although tremendous breakthroughs in shade varieties have been developed in the last few years. This grass prefers moderate to heavy fertilization and can be somewhat of a glutton when it comes to consumption of fertilizer. Without moisture Kentucky bluegrass has the unique ability to go dormant for long periods of time without any long term damage to the turf. Once the rains return the turf area will usually resume its green luster and appear that it was never stricken by drought. Since it is such a prolific spreader, the rhizomes on the plant aid in this recovery process and help to assure survival.

Rough-Stalked Bluegrass

A grass that is one of the few to prefer a shady location is called rough stalked bluegrass or Poa trivialis. Rough stalked bluegrass is unusual because it prefers cool, wet, and shady conditions. The only drawback from using this type of grass is that it cannot withstand drought conditions very well. Hot summers will kill this grass or thin out the grass very badly. Its usefulness should not be overlooked when using this variety in blends or mixtures. Rough stalked bluegrass is also commonly used in the south as a grass to overseed Bermuda grass on golf course fairways and athletic fields. The reason this is done is so that when the Bermuda grass starts to go dormant for the winter the rough stalked bluegrass can take over to give the area a playable surface. Also the rough stalked bluegrass is not too aggressive to allow the Bermuda to take back over in the spring. The rough stalked bluegrass cannot handle the heat so it basically dies out as the Bermuda grass reclaims the area for play during the normal season. It can be said that the rough stalked provides "good transition" as the seasons change. A popular variety of rough stalked bluegrass that is used is called "Sabre."

Perennial Ryegrass

Another very common cool season grass is Perennial Ryegrass or Lolium Perenne. Perennial Ryegrass can be found in lawns, athletic fields, and is very common in golf course fairways. This grass is usually grown in accompaniment with Kentucky bluegrass in most instances. The reason being is ryegrass is somewhat of a clump type grass and does not spread and fill in nearly as quickly as what bluegrass does. Ryegrass often has a darker color than bluegrass and can withstand mowing heights as low as a ½ inch if irrigated well and maintained correctly.

It is believed that this grass originated in the British Isles and was introduced to the U.S. many years after Kentucky bluegrass was used here. Perennial ryegrass thrives in moist soil conditions and is mostly a full sun grass type. It does require good fertility but has one of the natural dark green colors of any grass species when it is healthy and vigorously growing. The most useful characteristic of the ryegrass in general is the ability to germinate very quickly. This is one of the primary reasons the perennial ryegrass is used in seed mixtures along with other grasses. Since many other grasses are slow to germinate or establish the perennial, ryegrass can provide a cover crop, so to speak until the others catch up. The reason it is so common in athletic fields and golf courses is due to the ability to tolerate traffic and wear at lower growing heights. Irrigation is always helpful when keeping perennial ryegrass looking good because it thrives in moist conditions.

Tall Fescue

If there was ever a grass that was to be considered durable and versatile then it would be tall fescue. Tall fescue or Festuca arundinacea is the most adaptable grass species there is. It will grow in any soil condition including the worst clays. It used to be this species of grass in general was not planted for a desirable appearance but more for where and how it can be used. For years the highway departments have relied on tall fescue to establish medians and prevent erosion on highway projects. It has an excellent heat and drought tolerance and is resistant to most insect and fungus problems.

Fescue is a bunch type grass and the older varieties are not usually used where an aesthetically pleasing grass is desired. It has a clumpy or uneven appearance and does require a fairly high mowing height because of the large crowns that the grass has. Because of these large crowns it also has a rough feeling when it is walked on or driven over, much like that of old rough road. Tall fescue is not an aggressive spreader and only can spread by tillers. It has no ability to spread by rhizomes; therefore, if an area of turf is damaged it is difficult for fescue to repair itself to the condition before hand. This is also the reason that the grass is seeded at a very high rate because it cannot spread to fill itself in. If a pickup truck were to drive through an area that was covered with tall fescue and make ruts, those tracks would probably fill in with weeds or another grass type. Again this is because of the nature of fescue and its inability to spread on its own.

For that reason, it is very common for this tall fescue to be mixed with bluegrass in many cases.

Kentucky 31 is a tall fescue and not a bluegrass. For years, the Kentucky prefix has troubled home owners by the way it is promoted in retail trade. This is the oldest and most well known variety of the tall fescues. It is a forage grass and is reasonably inexpensive to buy which is why it has become so common over the years. Now in more recent years there are many newer varieties of tall fescue which are a little more desirable in appearance and in their growth habits.

Dwarf and Turf Type Fescues

More recent dwarf versions of fescue grass have been developed and are being used widely in the lawn and landscaping industry. These slower growing varieties are much denser in growth. They are now very common for golf course roughs and other turf applications. The only problem with them is since they are a slower growing plant type, recovery from injury is much slower as well. One way that researchers are dealing with this problem is by trying to breed the rhizome characteristics into fescues so that they will eventually be able to spread out on their own and the seed rates required for establishment will be much lower also. Dwarf fescues make wonderful lawns in most of the transition zone and can be used in parts of the North and South. Like their predecessors, the tall fescues, this type of grass will grow in a huge range of soil types and temperature conditions.

Fine Fescues

There are several different fine fescues known as the Festuca spp. This grass type is known for having fine hair-like characteristics and a delicate appearance. They adapt well to low fertility and can even tolerate a low ph. The fine fescues will grow in shade and can tolerate hard dry soils while still maintaining a decent appearance. These grasses are not really considered a stand-alone grass type and are usually always mixed in with other grass varieties. They do germinate fairly quickly and can be considered a starter grass over cover crop in their usefulness. Following is a list of cool season turf types:

- Kentucky Bluegrass
  - Dormancy during drought (Water glutton)
  - Mowing heights from 1½" to 3"
  - Good green color
  - Wide range in transition zone to North where this will grow
  - Good green color
  - Fine carpet like appearance
  - Requires a lot of fertilizer
- Rough Stalked Bluegrass
  - Grows well the shade
  - Works in seed mixtures
  - Transitions well in warm season grass as a cover grass
- Perennial Ryegrass
  - Very natural dark green color
  - Durable against foot traffic
  - Fast germination
  - Mixes well with other grasses
  - Clumpy appearance if not seeded heavy
- Tall Fescue
  - Drought tolerant
  - Traffic Tolerant
  - Grows on almost any soil type
  - Not a good lawn grass for closely mowed areas
  - Clumpy texture
  - Wide leaf blade
  - Does not spread well
- Dwarf or Turf Type Fescues
  - New varieties are exceptional for lawn use

- Drought tolerant
- Nice green luster and leaf shape
- Does not spread on its own
- Slow to repair from damage
- Fine Fescues
  - Really more of a mixture of blended grass
  - Grows well in shade
  - Can handle some dry poor soils
  - Can handle low fertility
  - Not a good stand alone turf type

WARM SEASON GRASSES

There are only a few warm season grasses that grow in the U.S. These grasses are only found in Southern climates and a portion of the lower half of the transition zone. The warm season grasses that do grow in the transition zone are often subjected to severe damage during the winter months due to the extreme cold conditions in the Midwest.

Zoysia Grass

Zoysia grass is for the most part the only warm season grass that is grown in the middle or Northern regions of the transition zone. Although it is cold tolerant and will come back from year to year it does stay in dormancy for long periods of time when planted in the transition zone. The three types of Zoysia that are grown in the U.S. are Zoysia japonica, Zoysia matrella, and Zoysia tenuifolia. Zoysia was originated in Japan.

The original cultivar for Zoysia that was used in the U.S. was one with the name "Meyer." It is still one of the most popular and readily available varieties on the market today. It is very drought tolerant and has a great color in season. It has also been proven to be the one of the coldest tolerant of the Zoysia species. Zoysia is also a very disease and insect free type of turf which requires little maintenance. Also since it is so aggressive and lush in the way that it grows,

TECH TIP
Thatch is the partially decomposed layer of organic matter that is situated above the ground.

weeds often have a hard time competing in a Zoysia lawn. It requires little water and only minimal fertilization to look good. It does tend to remain dormant for at least 6 months in the Northern regions but stays fairly active in the Southern States.

Sometimes Zoysia is sold in trade publications and popular magazines as a "wonder grass" that is too good to be true. Although this grass has some great characteristics, it is not as perfect as what some

FIGURE 2-4
This lawn actually has cool season grass on the right side and Zoysia grass on the other side. Warm and cool season grasses both can grow in the transition zone.

sales gimmicks make it out to be. If there is any major draw back to Zoysia it is the dormancy period that it has in most regions. Not only is the dormancy unsightly to look it but it can also create a fire hazard where if a cigarette butt was tossed out it could ignite an entire lawn. This grass type is also problematic when it comes to thatch problems. Thatch is the partially decomposed layer of organic matter that is situated above the ground. It can cause drainage problems and even nutrient availability problems for any and all turf-grasses, however warm season grasses tend to be worse for thatch problems. For the most part this is one of the biggest struggles with dealing with Zoysia. The other problem is that once Zoysia is established it can be somewhat evasive and almost impossible to get rid of if you ever decide to change grass types later on.

Bermuda Grass

Bermuda grass is a warm season grass that is very popular in the southern transition zone and almost all parts of the Southern states. In the northern parts of the transition zone and other regions of the country Bermuda is considered to be a weed. Cynodon dactylon as it is called botanically is a very useful grass for many stadiums and golf courses and many parts of the country. It has a very adaptable mowing height and can be cut anywhere from ⅛ inch on up to three inches.

It is believed that Bermuda grass actually got its origin somewhere in Africa. This grass type has excellent heat and drought tolerance that is even better than that of Zoysia. It adapts well to close mowings and can tolerate a wide range of soil types. The grass is very aggressive and recovers from damage quickly. It is not a cold tolerant grass however and is very susceptible to winter injury. This is why it is not considered a good grass to use very far North in the U.S.

The reason Bermuda grass is considered a weed in the North is due to the winter injury problem. Instead of thick thriving lawns like those seen in the South, small areas of Bermuda pop up here and there in the lawn. They are not really that noticeable in the well manicured areas until first frost when these areas become brown long before the rest of the lawn goes dormant.

A major disease problem that exists with lawns that are Bermuda is a disease called "spring dead spot." It is still somewhat of a mystery why exactly this disease occurs. Large dead areas develop in the turf through the summer months which can persist into fall and possibly even into the next season. The spots are ring like areas where all or most of the turf will die in the center.

The other problems that exist in Bermuda are the same as most of the warm season grasses. The grass is very evasive and can get out of control. Once established it can be hard to get eradicate. This is also a grass that can have problems with thatch. Also when Bermuda is planted in the transition zone a person can expect dormancy for 6 months of the year.

The newest and most successful forms of Bermuda that have been planted in recent years are referred to as the "tiff" series. There is "tiff-green," "tifway," and "tiflawn."

St. Augustine Grass

St. Augustine grass is an extreme Southern grass when grown in the United States. Stenotaphrum secundatum is the botanical name for St. Augustine grass. Although this grass is a common grass in the state of Florida it is not nearly as common in other parts of the U.S. It is used on both golf courses and residential lawns in all of Florida. It is not found in any other regions is because it is not cold tolerant at all. This has limited its progression north into other southern states. There are newer varieties of St. Augustine that can now be found in other southern regions but they still do not tolerate cold weather very well.

Two of most distinctive features of St. Augustine grass is the plush carpet feel it has under your feet when you walk on it and the aggressive way that the grass spreads using stolons. St. Augustine is the most aggressive spreader that exists. Since this grass does spread so rapidly edging sidewalks at the time of each mowing is a must. St. Augustine also has the capability to thrive in the poorest growing conditions. It will grow in salty conditions which are common to Florida since it is next to the ocean and it will even grow in dense shade. St. Augustine is a glutton for water and does require fertilizer. Mowing is needed sometimes less than every seven days when temperatures are right and moisture is abundant.

There is a disease that is worth mentioning that seems to be more common every year in St. Augustine grass. It is referred to as SAD or St. Augustine decline. It is typically a disease that shows up 4-5 yrs after establishment of a yard and is now being fought by simply using varieties that are resistant to this disease. "Raleigh" is a variety of St. Augustine that is showing great promise in resistance to SAD and also expanding the use of St. Augustine grass into other more Northern states.

Here is a review warm season turf types:

- **Zoysia**
  - Grows well into the northern transition zone
  - Old and reliable warm season grass type
  - Adapts well to variable mowing heights
  - Has thatch problems on a regular basis
  - Can be a fire hazard when dormant
  - Stays dormant for 6 months or more in Northern states

- **Bermuda grass**
  - Adapts to a huge range of mowing heights
  - Can be evasive in the way in grows and spreads (needs edged often)
  - Grows in huge parts of the South and transition zone
  - Requires little fertilizer in lawn conditions
  - Has some disease issues

- **St. Augustine grass**
  - Only grows in a small region in extreme Southern States
  - Has great color and texture
  - Somewhat an evasive spreader, needs edged weekly

- Low fertilizer needs
- High water requirement for good color

MIXTURES AND BLENDS

Grasses often do the best when they are put into a blend or mixture. A blend is a combination of 2 or more varieties of turfgrass within the same species. In other words you might have the variety of blue-grass called Pennstar™ blended in with another variety called Fly-king™. Both of these grasses are in the bluegrass family but have characteristics that make them more suitable when used together. The reason blends are used is due to the unique nature of each individual cultivar. A cultivar is a cultivated variety of a grass that is bred to have a specific trait. Some cultivars are genetically bred for color while other cultivars are meant to have disease resistance.

Mixtures of grasses are two completely different species of grasses used to get a desired effect. I have briefly mentioned how bluegrass and ryegrass often accompany one another in the locations they are used. The idea is very similar to that of a blend. When a couple of varieties are used in a location each variety can adapt to where it is most comfortable. For instance one species of grass may thrive in a shady location where another grass may prefer full sun.

Since either a blend or a mixture will contain different seed types and varieties the consumer should always read the seed label tag on every bag so they can identify these types. Every seed package is required to have a tag on it identifying the type of seed and the quality of seed as well. Make sure that the inert material in the bag is less than 2% and that the weed content is less than .1%. Good seed companies will produce seed with less than 1% inert and .05% weed content in some cases. The tag should also read "no noxious weeds." This simply means that you are not going to buy something loaded with evasive seeds in the mixture. Each variety or type of seed should be marked on the tag along with the percentage of that seed that is contained in the bag. Keep in mind seeds are different sizes and weights so the naked eye is a poor judge of content. Also since seeds are different sizes the percentage of weeds and inert should be much smaller when the seed sizes are smaller. You should always remember that if a seed bag is opened and not completely used you should always leave the tag attached until the bag is disposed of. This will avoid making costly mistakes and keep the misuse of turf species to a minimum.

Following is a review of steps for determining your lawn type:

- First find your geographic location on the U.S. hardiness zone map.

- Next figure out if you fall into the warm season, cool season, or transition zone map.

- Review the information about grass types to see what characteristics you might have currently.

- If you do not like your current grass type determine what characteristics you do want.

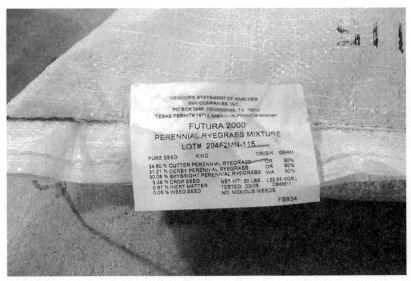

FIGURE 2-5
Perennial ryegrass seed tag.

- Make sure the grass you choose will grow in your climate.
- Make sure your grass is a newer variety (remember newer varieties typically possess the best characteristics).

3

Understanding and Preparing Soils

Having the perfect looking lawn is something that is achievable by anyone. The most important piece of that puzzle is to know and understand how soil can affect your goal. Soil is the basis for almost all living plant material in existence. If you are able to have an understanding of how soil can be manipulated and improved then the task of maintaining turf on that soil is much easier. All plants have basic criteria of needs for survival and most of these things are derived from the soil. Soil can be defined as natural bodies which most plants grow in.

TECH TIP
Soils can be defined as natural bodies which most plants grow in.

INTRODUCTION TO SOILS

Soils take on a wide range of characteristics and are different in almost every part of the world. There are clay soils, loam soils, basins, deserts and numerous other soil types. Each soil has a unique structure making it very different from one plot of ground to the next. Often soils can even vary in two locations on the same property. Many of the differences between soils come from the individual biological components of the soils. Some areas for instance that are high in limestone content may have a higher ph. A soil that is high in sand content or quartz may drain more quickly than another soil composed of clay.

All grass plants have specific requirements for healthy growth:

- Air
- Water
- Nutrients
- Light
- Heat
- Organic matter
- Mechanical support

Most of the items in this list are directly related to the type of soil you are trying to establish grass on. If any of these factors are not present a plant may not have the optimum growing conditions.

SOIL PH

The two basic elements for correcting soil for plant growth are ph and fertility. Although soils vary in every region, from a turfgrass standpoint, ph must be in a certain range and there must also be a certain level of nutrition available in the soil.

Ph is probably the number one factor for having healthy grass that is overlooked in the lawn care industry today. The reason ph is so crucial is due to the overall role soil ph plays. A soil that does not have the correct ph will not have the correct balance of any beneficial nutrients or organisms that are found in that soil. The optimum range for turfgrass is in the range of 6.2–7.0 on a Ph table. Turfgrass is probably the pickiest of all plants when it comes to the requirements of soil ph and the amount of each nutrient it requires.

There are also a wide range of microorganisms that live in the soil that help to improve soil structure and provide an optimum growing environment. These organisms will be in much smaller numbers in a soil that is not in that optimum range of 6.2–7.0. This is why it is so critical for a soil test to be done before you even think about improving or establishing new grass. Most ph

PRO POINTER

Ph is probably the number one factor for having healthy grass that is over looked in the lawn care industry today.

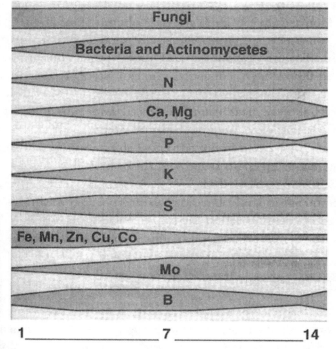

FIGURE 3-1

A lawn ph should range in the area of 6.2 to 7.0. This ph level provides the best soil condition for the encouragement of microorganisms and all other beneficial things that are found in the soil.

or fertility problems that might exist with your soil can be diagnosed right away with a simple soil test. Of any of the problems that exist in a lawn, a ph adjustment is probably the easiest to diagnose and correct. A soil test will reveal the ph of a lawn and any nutrient deficiencies that are present. This is a very inexpensive test and can usually be performed by a local co-op or state extension office. If the test indicates a low ph, less than 6.2, then a lime application will correct the problem. Lime, which is easy to apply and readily available in most regions, is an inexpensive product that will fix a low ph. It may be in different forms, or particle sizes, depending on the availability in a particular area. It is possible that a soil would test high on a ph chart, over 7.5, in some regions but it is very uncommon. If a soil test revealed a high ph, that would indicate a need for some sort of soil acidifier. Soil acidifiers are seldom needed in most situations. Also, if you want to make sure that your yard stays in good shape, a soil test should be performed about every three years to make sure that things are staying in balance.

Even though a lime application corrects a low ph, it will take several months before the actual ph of the soil will change. This is one reason why soil ph and fertility should be addressed in the fall. The fall is a great time for adjusting ph and applying fertilizers.

SOIL FERTILITY

Fertilizer is applied to provide nutrients to the soil that will be available for plants to take up through the roots. These nutrients are required for turfgrass plants to grow, maintain a green color, and reproduce.

The primary nutrients required by turfgrass are:

- Nitrogen
- Phosphorus

- Potassium (potash)

These three nutrients are called macronutrients and they need to be applied to turfgrass yearly in the form of some sort of fertilizer. These are the most common elements found in most fertilizers and will be shown on a fertilizer bag as N-P-K. Instead of the N, P, and K there will be three numbers in a ratio. The ratio of the three numbers represents the percentage of each element in the fertilizer. This is referred to as the analysis.

This is how a fertilizer analysis would appear on a bag of fertilizer:

(N-P-K)
28-6-12

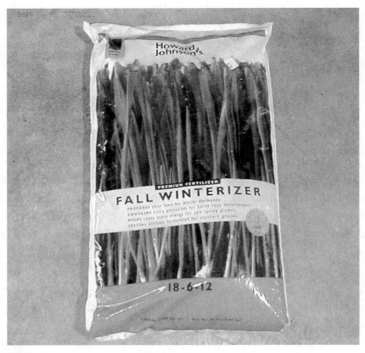

FIGURE 3-2
This fertilizer bag shows the analysis of how much N-P-K is in the contents clearly on the front.

The ratio of these numbers has to do with the percentages of each element that are actually in the fertilizer bag.

There are other nutrients which are found in some of the higher quality fertilizers which turfgrass requires in smaller amounts. The secondary nutrients needed for healthy grass are:

- Calcium

- Magnesium

- Sulfur

The last few elements that turfgrass requires are only needed in relatively low amounts and are called micronutrients or trace elements. The micronutrients needed for healthy grass are:

- Iron

- Manganese

- Boron

- Copper

- Zinc

- Molybdenum

- Chlorine

Micronutrients are not present in most fertilizers and are the least important in the overall health of turfgrass plants. However, a soil that is totally lacking in any element may reveal an odd characteristic of turf color or growth. It is the total arrangement of elements that makes up the balance of what a healthy grass plant will need to grow.

The soil test will provide a better insight to what nutrients you will need to apply to the soil and in what amounts. It is important to recognize that too much, or too little, of any fertilizer elements can provide and undesirable result.

Nitrogen is the most required element for healthy grass and needs to be applied in fairly large quantities to the turf on a yearly basis. This element is an essential component of chlorophyll and other plant substances. Since chlorophyll provides the green coloration that is seen in leaves, a plant low in nitrogen will not have a nice bright green color. It is possible, however, that if too much Nitrogen is applied to a lawn a burning (browing) of the turf can occur.

All fertilizers have a rate of N-P-K in their analysis as mentioned before. The ideal analysis of N-P-K should be in a ratio of 3-1-2 for most turf species. This is not always a guaranteed fix for a fertility problem and there are many different fertilizers and analysis that exist. Special fertilizers with unusual analysis are needed for circumstances when a soil test might reveal a specific need. What to remember when buying a fertilizer:

- Try and purchase fertilizers that show they are slow release on the bag.

- Make sure that you try to get close to a 3-1-2 ratio for a general purpose fertilizer. Note: This is not the analysis to use when treating with a chemical on the fertilizer such as a pre-emergent or weed killer. (See Chapter 8 for more information)

- Look for a fertilizer that has micronutrients. The micronutrients might be the thing that will give your yard an edge over the neighbor's lawn.

- Remember that the time to apply fertilizer has nothing to do with when a major retail store has fertilizer on sale.

SOIL TYPES

Soils are all composed of minerals and materials that been here for thousand of years. A mineral soil is composed of four major components:

- Inorganic or mineral materials
- Organic matter
- Water
- Air

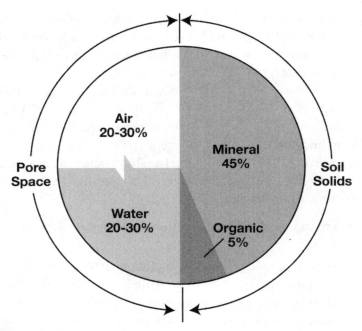

FIGURE 3-3
Soil composition circle.

All soils have these components in them at some level or another. It is the variation of these four components that creates soil types.

All soils have a different content of organic or inorganic materials. These materials are arranged in different proportions of variably sized particles. This property is referred to as soil texture. The terms sandy, silty, or loam are referring to various categories of soil texture. These references are describing a specific soil structure, texture, and composition.

The three major types of inorganic soil particles are sand, silt, and clay. These particles compose the majority of any soils composition. Not all three types will necessarily be found in one soil or region. Soils will have different quantities of those materials along with the water, air and the organic particles. The organic particles found in soils are in much smaller quantities. Usually organic con-

Table 3-1
Organic soil properties.

General Properties/Three Major Organic Soil Particles	Range in diameter/particles in (mm)		
Property	Sand	Silt	Clay
	(0.052mm)	(0.002-0.05mm)	(<0.002mm)
Means of observation	Naked Eye	Microscope	Electron Microscope
Dominant minerals	Primary	Primary & Secondary	Secondary
Attraction of particles to each other	Low	Medium	High
Attraction of particles to water	Low	Medium	High
Ability to hold chemical nutrients & Supply them to plants	Very Low	Low	High
Consistency properties when wet	Loose, Gritty	Smooth	Sticky,plastic
Consistency properties when dry	Very loose,gritty	Powdery,some clods	Hard Clods

tent in a soil is as low as 1%-6% of the soils total composition. Organic matter is very beneficial to soil and can be added to almost any soil type to improve the soil structure and texture. Examples of organic matter are:

- Leaves
- Peat moss
- Compost

Almost all plants prefer soils high in organic matter which is especially true for grasses. All of the components of soil are connected in the way they affect one another. A very organic loamy type soil for instance will have more air spaces and better water retention compared to that of a sandy soil which will have good air space but be very poor at water retention.

A very helpful tool in analyzing soil composition is the soil textural triangle. The soil textural triangle is a descriptive tool created to help label various soil types according to their composition. The soil types are based on the quantities of sand, silt, and clay present in the soil. These descriptions are used by all soil scientists to describe soils in every region of world. Every soil that exists will fall somewhere in the category of the soil triangle diagram.

Recognizing the soil type and composition of soil will help you develop a better understanding of how to maintain the plants that are growing in the soil. By understanding that a sandy soil will need more water than a clay soil, you will have a better understanding on how to care for your own lawn. The differences in soil structure require that certain cultural practices be followed in order to maximize efficiency and minimize expense.

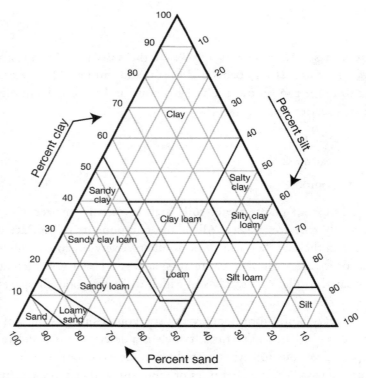

FIGURE 3-4
Textural triangle.

The presence of air in the soil is critical to a turfgrass plants survival by allowing the plant to get oxygen, water, and nutrients to the roots. Soil that is compacted will be very low in porosity, which

TECH TIP
Yards that are aerated on a yearly basis are much healthier and look better than lawns that are not aerated.

often occurs in clay soil types. If you notice that your lawn has areas that are compacted then those areas need some correcting. There are ways to improve a soil and allow more air to get into the soil. Any improvements made to increase soil porosity will help to reduce turf stress and damage. This in turn will provide a healthier growing environment for the plants. Yards that are aerated on a yearly basis are much healthier and look better than lawns that are not aerated.

Aeration of the soil is one way to achieve this air exchange and is any mechanical way to improve the aeration in the soil. This allows better porosity and ventilation within the soil. The idea is to increase the plants ability to be able to take up nutrients and water that are needed for survival. Soils can become "sealed" up to the point where there is little moisture or fertilizer content penetrating the soil. This is when some sort of aeration will improve the growing environment and is especially true for clay type soils.

Aeration does not have to be man made or done mechanically, as there are also many natural forms of aeration. The most recognized form of natural aeration is earth worm activity. You may complain about the bumps or lumps that are caused from earthworms in your yard but this is nature's way of allowing the air exchange with the soil.

Soil contains almost everything that a grass plant needs to grow, develop, and establish itself. This is why the maintenance and care of the soil is often as important as maintenance of the plants that grow in the soil. Plants get all of the moisture and nutrients they need for survival right out of the ground. Without moisture or nutrition in the ground soil does little more than hold the plant up and support it. It is the combination of soil and plant care that will make your lawn a true success. Steps for taking care of the soil in your lawn follow:

1. Determine what type of soil you have in your yard and what problems you might be able to correct:

   - Poor drainage

   - Compacted soils

   - Possible Ph or fertilizer problems

2. Send in a soil sample to your local co-op or extension agency.

3. Evaluate the results and talk to your extension office if necessary to interpret your results.

4. Apply lime and fertilizer if needed based on those soil sample results. (Please refer to Chapter 8 for more detailed information on how and when fertilizers should be used)

4

Irrigation and Watering Practices

All plants are composed mostly of water, and turfgrass in general is a plant that has a high need for water. Plants like humans have a certain requirement for moisture to maintain a healthy state and to survive. Without water, over time turfgrass plants can die. Most grass plants do have the ability to go without water for periods of time in a state known as dormancy but even then there are limitations to a plants recovery when they are deprived of water for sustained periods of time.

There is a time frame where all plants can recover from a lack of moisture. Dormancy in grass is a natural response and the dormancy period can be sustained for a few weeks at a time. There is also a point where a plant cannot recover from moisture loss, this is known as the permanent wilting point. Plant cells have a unique ability to regenerate from moisture loss up to a certain point. Plant cells can become dried out which can make the grass look wilted or even dead looking. Amazingly enough, once the plant is exposed to moisture again, the plant cells become turgid again, and before long it is hard to tell that there was any moisture stress at all.

PRO POINTER
The permanent wilting point is where a grass plant cannot recover from moisture loss.

Not all turfgrass plants need equal amounts of water nor do they need to have water everyday for most species. For example, a lawn could contain the same type of turf over the entire yard, but only part of the yard may have a need for water. The same can be said for areas of the lawn that may contain a certain grass type versus another area of the lawn which may be composed of completely different grass. The reasons a yard might be dry in some areas could be caused by:

- Differences in soil types
- Amount of shade on one part of the lawn compared to the other
- Slope or grade of the property
- Drainage problems
- Tree roots
- Use of the turf area and traffic on the turf
- Cultural practices and maintenance

If your yard does have inconsistencies with moisture and appears stressed from time to time you may be a candidate for an irrigation system. Irrigation is not for everyone but if you desire the perfect lawn then an irrigation system will be a key component to having a successful lawn experience. A yard without adequate water is sure to have times when it does not look green and lush. By being able to water the grass you are also able to assist fertilizers and other chemicals in their job.

TYPES OF IRRIGATION SYSTEMS

One major problem with modern irrigation systems is that they continue to become more complex each and every year. My first recommendation would be to hire a professional if you have questions about tackling a difficult project. Newer state of the art irrigation systems have plumbing and electrical components that require knowledge and skill to install. Newer systems are even utilizing high tech computer components that allow the systems to be turned on by a computer or even a cell phone. If the idea of doing the installation yourself sounds overwhelming to you, but at the same time irrigation is something you would be interested in, then call a reputable landscape or lawn care professional to see about irrigation systems in your area. There are many companies that specialize in irrigation only and that might be your only hope to get the latest state of the art type irrigation systems.

Older irrigation system technology is still available which might be more suited for your needs. A very basic system can be set up by a homeowner and maintained quite easily. A typical system I would recommend for most yards would be a pop up mist or a pop up rotary style system that utilizes a simple timer device that can easily be set to run with minimal effort on your part. The ease of use of the system is unfortunately the driving force behind the newer systems being so complex. Ideally you will want an irrigation system to be somewhat simple in design and helpful enough to take care of your watering needs without you having to "baby-sit" the watering process.

A key decision maker for your irrigation needs might have to first start with your local city ordinances and laws. It is true that in some parts of the country irrigation use is limited because of water shortages and abuse of water use. Step one in the decision making process should be to see if your city has any restrictions on installation of an irrigation system. It is even possible that you might be allowed to put in an irrigation system but not be allowed to use it in a drought scenario. This is especially true for areas that often have limited rain fall because irrigation is viewed as wasteful.

A possible limiting factor to irrigation installation could be the water pressure of your city's water supply. You might want to see if there are other irrigation systems

> **PRO POINTER**
> Make sure you shop around from company to company and ask the right questions. Prices can vary by the thousands of dollars based on components.

in your community and find out if there were any problems when they installed their system. It is not to say you cannot install irrigation without sufficient water pressure, but you will have to consider a more complex system with an external pump. Anytime there is complication with the installation process there will be added cost and more maintenance.

A pop up rotary type system can be fairly easy to install and many of the "mass merchants" now provide kits that include sprinkler heads, pipe, and timers all in the same box. All pop up heads can vary with the pipe size used to install the head, so there is nothing set in stone as to what to expect from system to system. Pop up rotary heads use water pressure to force the sprinklers to turn while dispersing water out of both sides of the sprinkler. You will want to arrange the heads to provide overlapping coverage that does not leave any area untouched. More advanced systems can allow you to run only part of the system at one time or even just one sprinkler, but a basic system will not provide you with those types of features.

FIGURE 4-1
Rotary type sprinkler systems are common for lawns, athletic fields, and even golf courses.

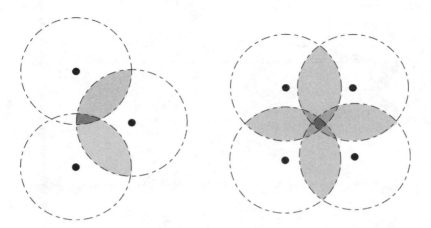

FIGURE 4-2
The image on the left shows a triangular configuration with sufficient overlap, where the image on the right shows more of a square pattern. Your needs will vary based on the shape of the lawn.

There are specific ways to calculate the coverage area of a pop up rotary system, but some of them require an engineer's hand in the calculations. This is once again why you may want to leave this up to the professionals. As a homeowner you can only calculate the range of the heads you are installing and make sure that there is sufficient overlap with the system you are using. Sprinklers should provide adequate coverage but at the same time not be saturating an area from too much water.

The pressure of your system will have a lot to do with how your system will perform whether you have installed it yourself or not. Sprinkler heads are all designed to perform in a certain range of water pressure. If the pressure is too low or too high the amount of water applied will not be uniform, and the grass may show problems from over or under watering.

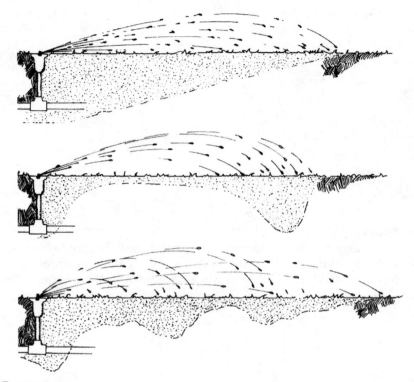

FIGURE 4-3
A. Correct pressure
B. Under Pressure
C. Over pressure

Installation of irrigation lines is the most difficult part of the installation process. A professional will have specialized tools that can easily bury the lines to the proper depth with one or two passes. If you are doing the project yourself you will have to consider renting a trenching device to install the lines. Primary lines will be larger than the lines running to the individual heads, so the trench width can vary from system to system. Keep in mind that back filled soil can settle after the lines are installed, so you may have to fill in low spots if the lines settle any. If you are looking to install a system in a new lawn situation then it always best to put the system in prior to seeding or sodding.

It is also critical that you consider the frost line in your area and how frost can affect your irrigation system. Typically, irrigation systems are drained soon enough in the year that frost is not a concern for shallow lines, but there are major concerns with frost the further north you are in the United States. Frost can cause lines to crack or explode from the freezing and thawing effect.

Pop up type systems can utilize spray heads in any size and water volume. The important part is that the coverage of the system is adequate enough to get enough moisture to all of the grass you are trying to get water to. Not all of the grass needs the same amount of water which is when more modern systems give you the benefit of only using part of the system instead of the entire system. There are several reasons even the best planned systems may not cover the lawn equally:

- Different sprinkler head styles
- Wear of the sprinkler heads
- Size of the lines
- Pressure of the system
- Grade of the lines the water is moving through (trying to push water up hill)

Any one of these factors can create inconsistency with your water coverage which could cause you to over water or under water the desired coverage area.

Timers are important to the success of your irrigation system. You must consider that timers can get out of time to where the irrigation system is running too long or not long enough. You must consider the type of timer you have and realize that digital or more modern systems are prone to resetting. Older clock type timers did not get out of time because they worked on more of a clock type of principle that was not disrupted by power outages. This will all be part of the maintenance required to keep your irrigation system working properly.

MAINTENANCE

The key to a good lawn is maintenance, and the key to keeping an irrigation system working is no different. Maintenance of an irrigation system can keep you from costly repairs down the road. Maintenance will need to be done on a weekly, if not a monthly, basis. Heads need to be cleaned out from time to time and adjustments will need to be made to make sure that your coverage area stays consistent during the irrigation season. Following are some tips:

- At the start of the season you will need to fill the irrigation lines and test each sprinkler to see that they are working correctly.

- Sprinklers should be checked for overlap and adjusted to cover the grass you need to get water to.

- Weekly inspections of the timer system should be done and you should always check to make sure that the heads all pop up and rotate correctly.

- You should walk the lines that lie under the lawn to make sure there are no leaks or problems that you cannot see.

- Make sure irrigation heads have not been hit by mowers or torn up from vandalism.

- Make sure drains in the system work correctly in case of a problem.

- Never forget to winterize your system in the winter which will require air to be blown through the lines and the water to be completely drained before temps get below freezing.

You can see that the maintenance of an irrigation system is never ending, but what if you do have a problem? This is when there may be a need to dig up lines or even replace heads from time to time. If you plan on doing the maintenance yourself you will need to have knowledge of basic plumbing and in some cases even electricity. Any time you add water and electricity together you are going to have problems at some point.

You need to really be prepared to care for an irrigation system if you choose to have irrigation. It is hard to have a perfect lawn without a supplemental water source during dry periods. You should consider if the work associated with irrigation is worth your desire to keep that green luster throughout the growing season. A big factor with having irrigation is the cost of putting in such a system. This does not end with the completion of the installation of the irrigation system. Here is a list of a few things that you can count on being a constant expense with your irrigation system:

- Cost of operation of the system: You can count a on a very high water bill and an increase in your electric bill from the daily and weekly operation of the irrigation system.

- Mowers can damage sprinkler heads and at some point heads are going to wear out. It would be good to budget for expected and unexpected damage to sprinkler heads.

- It may be necessary to dig up an extensive part of your irrigation lines if a leak develops. This could require some seeding or sodding of the area that is damaged from the leak. This tends to be one of the most expensive maintenance issues.

- Do not forget about winterization. If you are able to winterize your system yourself you could save some money but beware; One mistake could cause thousands of dollars in damage should water freeze in your irrigation system. Once again, if in doubt, you should leave it to the professionals.

You may want to also consider an anti-siphoning device. It is important to protect water sources from contamination if the supply is associated with a municipal water supply or a domestic well. In cases like these, a cross connection control device is desirable, and likely required, by local plumbing code. Reverse siphoning or 'backflow' occurs when a sudden drop in pressure is sustained (such as the failure of a water main) within the supply system. This can create a situation where contaminated water could seep back into the main water supply. As a homeowner you may not possess the knowledge and skill required to get into such a major plumbing project. Remember, if laws and ordinances exist, you will have to comply with these devices or skip using irrigation all together.

EMISSION DEVICES

A pop up rotary system is for sure the easiest to install and maintain of all of the irrigation types. You do need to be aware that there are three basic types of irrigation that could be used for a lawn system. The three basic systems you will find in lawns are fixed spray, rotor spray, and flood bubblers. Fixed spray heads are typically termed 'pop-ups,' as the nozzle pops up from 4" to 12" depending upon the application. They are commonly used in relatively narrow (16 feet or less) or irregularly shaped areas because of the design flexibility they offer. Rotors feature a rotating nozzle, so they are more useful in larger areas than in smaller areas. Many varieties are produced, to

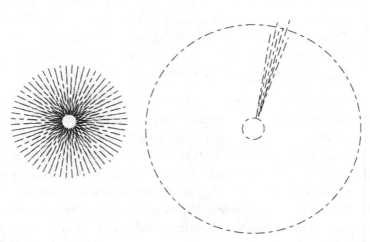

FIGURE 4-4
Pop up rotary pattern vs. a pop up mist type system.

work in areas as narrow as 16 feet. Larger units have a radius of throw that exceeds 80 feet. These often are used in golf courses so you would seldom see such applications in a residential setting. Flood bubblers are usually utilized to provide supplemental tree irrigation,

> **DID YOU KNOW?**
> Weeds can really take over a lawn if grass becomes weak from water stress, disease, or insects.

or in the landscaping, but these types of systems often tie in with the lawn irrigation system.

There is a new emphasis on water conservation sweeping the industry that is changing the way people view their irrigation needs. It is important to be water conscious even if you do not choose to install an irrigation system. Irrigation is not a necessity but more of a luxury for a vast part of the United States. This is not true in the Southwest and other regions where grass would not even grow without irrigation help, but overall grass does not need irrigation to survive from year to year. The balancing act comes into play with the sacrifices you make with your lawn from not having a good water source.

Grass that is in need of water is not considered thriving and healthy. Turf will have a much harder time competing with weeds and looking great with a lack of water. Weeds can really take over a lawn if grass becomes weak from water stress, disease, or insects. Be prepared for weeds to infest lawns if the grass goes dormant and it is not able to compete during dry times of the year. Weeds have much larger root zones and they are able to find water when your grass cannot. You must anticipate and tolerate a drier and potentially weedy lawn during the middle of the summer if you have not given the lawn any water to ease the stressed conditions.

Also consider that water stressed turf is more prone to disease and insect problems if it is suffering from water stress. Water stress can put the plant in a weakened state where, if infected by a

> **PRO POINTER**
> Also consider that water stressed turf is more prone to disease and insect problems.

pathogen or insect, the damage can be quite significant. If you have a problem with an insect or fungus, treatments can also be more difficult without irrigation. For example, the effectiveness of a grub control can be significantly better if you have the ability to irrigate slightly before and after the application of a granular product.

You should have a concept of the water usage from your irrigation system. There is a certain amount of water that should be applied for each type of turf type. Bluegrass is a bit of a glutton for water compared to fescue, so the irrigation needs would not need to be nearly as high. Your irrigation system output can easily be measured with the help of the household rain gauge. By using the rain gauge you can get an understanding of your system output. At least then you can determine how long your watering time should be. For most turf .1 inches of moisture per day will sustain the turf unless temps exceed 85–90 degrees F. At that point the irrigation amount may need to be increased to .15–.2 inches of moisture per day. These are only rules of thumb and irrigating every other day at times has major benefits to the grass. It is a better idea to water exhausted soils instead of exhausted plants. Even though your soil may seem dry, your grass plants can find moisture much easier than you would expect.

The amount of water needed can vary due to:

- Soil type
- Grade of property/runoff
- Turf type
- Irrigation output per sprinkler

The critical thing to remember when calculating your output of the irrigation system is that not every head will emit the same amount of water even if they are identical heads. This is why you must move the rain gauge around the lawn and take averages of the entire irrigation area. Make sure you have an average representation of the entire property. Usually heads that are down hill or in lower points will emit more water than head on hills or high spots.

There are signs of stressed turf to look for that can help you determine when your water system should be running:

- Yellow or purple colored grass

- Browning turf

- Thinning grass

A practice known as "syringing the grass" can help to reduce stress during hot and dry days with high temperatures. When temps are above 85 degrees you can save a lot of grass damage by turning on the water for a few seconds to cool off the grass leaves. Watch out for scorching which can occur if the water has run too long or grass becomes wet. The idea is to create a quick misting of the turf to cool off the air and grass surface.

Water in the early morning whenever possible and if you have a good timer then set it so it runs closer to the morning versus running in the evening. You should never water in the evening if it is avoidable because turf that stays wet through the night is much more likely to develop a disease. This is especially true during hot periods with high humidity. You will eventually get a feel for how your irrigation system performs and how to manage your water usage. Your turf quality will be considerably better by keeping turf wet enough to stay green, but yet dry enough to be healthy. It is very easy to over water a lawn, so do not think that a lot of water is always helpful.

No matter what you decide about installing an irrigation system, in most cases you are better off leaving a majority of the installation process up to someone else. It will be easy enough for you to maintain the system throughout the growing season, but at the end of the year you might be wise to get a professional to winterize your system and give it a once over look to make sure your maintenance has been adequate enough.

> **DID YOU KNOW?**
> Turf that stays wet through the night is much more likely to develop a disease.

5

Creating Lawn From Seed

When you look out into your yard do you see a lawn that is worn out, full of weeds, which needs to be reseeded? Creating a new lawn from seed is not as difficult as you may think. Also you can correct many other lawn problems while you are redoing the lawn from seed. The establishment period for turfgrass is the most critical time frame to insure the long term health of the grass plants, so you want to make sure you get it right the first time. The establishment period is when you have your best opportunity to create a healthy growing environment for the rest of the lawn's lifespan. This will be the time to address problems like soil fertility, ph, and the grade of the lawn.

LAWN RESEEDING

Following are steps for lawn reseeding:

1. Evaluation of the lawn

2. Evaluation of the soil and soil test

3. Spray to kill the old existing lawn to rid of any weeds or undesirable grasses

4. Incorporate materials such as organic matter, pelletized lime, or fertilizer to improve the soil with a tilling process. *Note There may need to be a step added to use a roller on very loose soils if you are not planning to use a drilling device that will help to level things out.

5. Grading of the soil to level the lawn if needed

6. Spread or drill the seed into the yard

7. Cover the seed with straw

8. Irrigate the area to insure a successful stand

SEEDING AND RE-ESTABLISHMENT OF TURFGRASS

> **DID YOU KNOW?**
> Any lawn that is more than 50% full of weeds would be considered to be at the point of starting over from scratch.

Seeding projects may be necessary for a couple of reasons. The first might be that you have an area that has never been seeded in grass before and now you want to turn this area into lawn. The other scenario might be that there is already existing turf in a particular area and you want to start over with new grass due to the poor condition of the existing grass. In either instance seeding is the best solution to your problem. Seeding can be easy to do and it is very cost effective compared to the use of sod.

When it comes to assessing the circumstances with your seeding project there must be a series of questions to think about when determining what will need to be done:

• Have I had a soil test?

• What improvements will need to be done to the soil?

• How will these improvements be done?

- Will there be irrigation or water available to the area?

- What will insure the long term success of the grass we are trying to grow in this location?

PRO POINTER
The only way to determine Ph and soil fertility needs is through the use of a soil test.

- What type of grass do we desire in this location?

This preliminary evaluation process could be compared to that of a site analysis that a landscape professional might use when assessing the landscaping around a new home. All factors for success of your new grass need to be considered. Things should be looked at like soil type, drainage, light, wind, and all other environmental factors that exist in the location. By doing this evaluation process more effective methods can be used during the establishment process.

One key step in the evaluation process is to get a soil test and review those results very carefully. Most soil tests for turf will give a basic analysis which will be fine for your purposes. A soil test will tell you several key principles for good lawn success:

- Ph of the soil

- Fertility needs of the soil (typically N-P-K)

- Organic matter content

The Ph of the soil is very critical to good turf success. The soil ph can affect everything else about your soil and it is even tied to soil fertility. The soil Ph should be in the level of 6.2-7.0 for ideal growing conditions for turfgrass. Most clay soils in the Midwest tend to be low in Ph. This is when a pelletized or agricultural lime would need to be applied to the lawn area to correct a below normal Ph. It is rare to have a high Ph but there are soil acidifiers that can be applied to correct those problems also. Ph is the balancing system for all of the micro-organisms and

TECH TIP
Soil Ph can affect everything in the soil like the ability of the grass to even be able to utilize all of the fertilizer that is present in the soil.

PRO POINTER
Fertilizers like lime work much faster when incorporated into the soil.

beneficial things that exist in the soil. Soils that are not balanced in Ph do not possess the qualities for the perfect lawn.

The soil test will also show what elements of fertilizer need to be added to meet the ideal grass growing conditions. A basic soil test shows the needs for N-P-K (Nitrogen, Phosphorus, and Potassium) which are the main Macro nutrients needed for healthy turfgrass. These three elements will be the only ones shown in the average soil test. It is possible that your soil test can show more specific results or that a more elaborate soil test can be performed. Even improving the basic elements will really allow your grass to thrive once it is planted. Fertilizers and lime will work much faster when incorporated into the soil.

Lime and fertilizer elements should be added during the soil preparation stage. It is the soil preparation process that will make the addition of soil amendments successful. Tilling is the best method for incorporating soil elements because you can get them into the soil profile several inches so they affect the soil immediately. Tilling will also allow you to incorporate organic matter into the soil. Organic matter is very helpful in loosening up hard and compacted soils. Organic matter allows roots to grow and spread out in the soil and it also improves moisture retention in the soil. There are several types of organic matter that can be used to improve your soils. Some examples of organic matter that can be tilled into the soil are:

- Peat moss
- Leaves
- Compost
- Manure/Compost
- Decomposed mulch or wood chips (must be decomposed)

REMOVING OLD TURF

The critical step to starting over is to make sure that the problems you have with the old lawn are gone for good. There might have been

FIGURE 5-1
This bale of peat moss can help loosen hardened soils if it is tilled into the soil during the preparation process.

a weed in your lawn that you just never could get under control or a type of grass that you never did care for. Now is the time to eliminate those problems once and for all. This can be quickly and easily done with a Roundup™ application over the entire area you want to seed. Roundup™ is an insurance policy to make sure that you have rid your yard of all of the older weedy vegetation once and for all. Keep in mind Roundup™ is a contact herbicide that will not leave any harmful residues to keep you from doing your seeding project right away. Roundup™ is a "here today, gone tomorrow" chemical that will not cause problems when used for this purpose. You should also know that the chemical name for Roundup™ is glyphosate and it can be purchased under many other trade mark names that might be less expensive. I do suggest allowing a complete burn down effect or the browning of all of the vegetation which will take a few days. This allows for easier tilling and a better chance to kill all of the weedy species. Allowing burn down is not always a possibility due to time constraints and it is ok to till the day after the area is sprayed. Another reason this step should be done is because some more evasive species of weeds can actually thrive from some sort of cultivation, such as tilling, by cutting them into pieces that will re-root and spread.

SOIL PREPARATION

If the area you are planning to establish grass on is deficient in a nutrient then it should be corrected at this stage. You can refer to your soil test to tell how deficient your soil might be. A soil test will

FIGURE 5-2
Ground ivy is a type of weed that can root if it is cut up during the cultivation process.

reveal the answers to successful turf establishment by telling you how much of an element should be added to get the soil to an acceptable level for grass establishment. Fertilizers can be applied over the soil with a rotary or drop type spreader. Rotary spreaders are much better for spreading materials

DID YOU KNOW?
Roundup™ is a contact herbicide that will not leave any harmful residues. You can begin your seeding project immediately after application.

compared to a drop spreader. They create less overlap and a much more even pattern for product dispersion. If you are having problems with wind when you are trying to spread fertilizer you can set the spreader at a half rate setting and go over the area in two different directions.

Do not forget about the Ph if your soil tests low. Spreading lime and incorporating it into the soil will need to be done during this stage for the best and fastest results. The soil test will show exactly how much lime should be added in order to correct Ph issues. Remember, lime is only a cure for Ph problems where the soil tests below a level of 6.2.

You are at an advantage to till nutrients into the soil instead of trying to add fertilizers or lime to the soil over established grass. By tilling in an element, or nutrient, the improvement to the soil is more immediate. When all of these nutrients are mixed into the soil there is more of an instant availability to the grass, as well as a fluffing of the soil that can be gained by tilling. The tilling action of the soil loosens soil particles and gives seedling grass a better chance to root into the soil.

If the soil test reveals a need for the addition of fertilizer, make sure you are using a starter fertilizer if possible. An example might be a 12-28-16; notice the lower first number and higher second number. This is telling you that there is a low amount of nitrogen and a high amount of phosphorus. New grass seedlings that are trying to establish roots require a high quantity of phosphorus for root stimulation. A lot of nitrogen is not needed because roots are what are desired, not tip growth. If the young grass plants get too much nitrogen then they

FIGURE 5-3
The process of using a rotary tiller, such as a Befco™ tiller behind a tractor, is one way to get soil amendments into the soil profile.

can become leggy or spindly in appearance. If you do not have access to a starter fertilizer then a general purpose 13-13-13 agriculture type fertilizer can work which is available at almost any place that sells fertilizer.

Tilling can be done with any type of rotary type tiller. Rear tine tillers and tractor mounted tillers are much easier to use than front tine tillers but any kind of tiller will work. Tilling does not have to be deep in the soil for grass establishment. Deep tilling can make the ground more difficult to level out but it can be more helpful in mixing the nutrients into the soil. If the soil is very fluffy and loose it might need to be lightly rolled in order to level the ground out for

FIGURE 5-4
An example of a fertilizer that would be used for a seeding project.

seeding preparation. Do not use a heavy roller, you do not want to over compact the soil you just loosened up. Avoid using a roller if possible if you have access to a drilling type of seeder. A slit seeder or drill type seeder will tend to level as it goes.

This is also the point in which to correct grading issues in the lawn. Since you have loosened the soil it is easy to redistribute the soil to areas where it is needed. Low spots that hold water or cause problems mowing should be filled. It is also important to get the grade of the soil to slope away from the house or landscaping. It is always a good idea to have water running away from your home or business instead of towards it. Minor grading issues can be fixed with a garden rake by moving and leveling soil out by hand. Larger grading issues will require a harrow or maybe even a tractor depending on the severity of the grade problems or the size of the area you are seeding. Larger seeding projects will require a compact tractor with an implement type of attachment in order to get the best results. There are many more equipment options when it comes to smaller residential sized lawns.

PLANTING THE SEED

The next step is to seed the area that has been prepared. It is possible to seed a yard with a spreader of some type, whether it is a drop spreader or rotary style. You probably will have just applied a fertilizer of some kind and possibly lime with a spreader of this type. If no mechanical renovation or tilling has been performed to the turf, over seeding with a spreader has very limited success. Spreading seed with a spreader only will leave seed on the surface of the ground where it is subject to many possible scenarios. The seed may be tracked off with foot traffic by humans or pets. In some instances birds will actually consume a portion of the seed before it germinates. Also, in general, a large portion of the seed simply will just not germinate at all because it never had the opportunity for the seed-to-soil contact that is required for it to grow. It can take a lot higher amount of seed to produce a desirable effect if you are just throwing seed on top of the ground. Seeding results are much better when a mechanical seeder is used.

The most common method for seeding is to use some sort of a seeding device that is engine driven or that fits on a tractor. The size of the project at hand will have a lot to do with what type of machine is being used. There are many types and styles of seeders available. There are roller type seeders, which I refer to as "non-powered seeders." A non-powered seeder is a seeder that usually will have a drop box for the seed that is followed by some sort of a large roller that will help to press the seed into the soil. These are almost always tractor mounted seeders because of the weight needed for the seeders to be effective.

A powered seeder can have either an engine or a PTO (power take off) to operate a slicing device of some sort. Much like that of a power rake there are usually knifes involved that will slice the soil while depositing seed from a seed box at the same time. A powered

FIGURE 5-5
This Sukup™ seeder is an example of a seeder that fits on a tractor but is driven by rolling on the ground.

seeder works much like what a crop drill would. The only difference is that the grass is the crop that is being planted. There are many small walk behind type seeders as well as larger tractor mounted seeders. Good brands of large powered seeders will usually have a large roller on the back to roll the seed into the soil to maximize seed germination. There are companies out there that claim to have one step seeding machines that till, drill, and roll all in one pass. From my experience their effectiveness has not been as remarkable as claimed and they are very pricey to own or rent.

FIGURE 5-6
This Ryan™ seeder works much like a large tractor-powered
seeder but is small enough to walk behind.

By using a seeder to drill the seed in some way, the soil is also
rolled out as the seed is being deposited. Using a rotary spreader to
spread the seed does nothing to level the freshly tilled soil which is
another reason to use a seeding device. If you are walking on freshly
tilled ground then you would have to worry about foot tracks. If a
tractor is used for the project and the seeder is not wide enough to
cover the tire tracks, then there can also be ruts to contend with.
There is the possibility though for using a turf roller or pull behind
roller to level out the soil if a rotary spreader was used. These are
somewhat effective for leveling on small projects where walk behind

equipment was used but not so good when it comes to removing large tractor ruts or tracks.

The seeding should be drilled in a way to minimize tracking to provide the smoothest possible result. Once the lawn has grown in and is ready for mowing it is often hard to correct uneven conditions at that stage. The more you can do to reduce traffic on newly seeded lawns the better off the grass will be. This goes for before, after, and during a seeding project. Keep in mind also that moist or wet soil may compact worse than what dry soils do. Also wet soils are more likely to be tracked or rutted during the seeding process.

Seeding with a drill should be done by covering the ground in a bi-directional pattern to insure good coverage in the end. This is really the best way to spread fertilizers, dry chemical, or seed. By cutting the rate in half and going over the area in two different directions you help to reduce skipped areas or places that might not have been reached while going over the area the first time. Also in the case of seeding with a tractor this might help to further cover up any tire tracks.

For example, you are seeding a football field and you are pulling a seeder over the area that has slicing knifes on three inch centers. This will mean that a majority of the seed will end up growing in those grooves but at a distance of three inches apart. You cut that rate in half and put down half of the seed running one direction and the other half running the other direction (much like a tic tac toe board). This will provide the best result when it grows in and make a much denser surface to start out with. In the case of using fescue, which if you remember is a non-spreading turf, there may be the need to go over the top of the area with a rotary spreader even after the seed is drilled. This will help to eliminate bare or skipped areas from the seeder spacing and allow a more dense coverage.

Many people unfortunately look at the bottom number being the price of the seed. This is unfortunate because seed comes in a wide variety of types and qualities. Blends and mixtures will work

TECH TIP
The best way to drill seed is to go over the ground in a cris-cross pattern to insure good coverage.

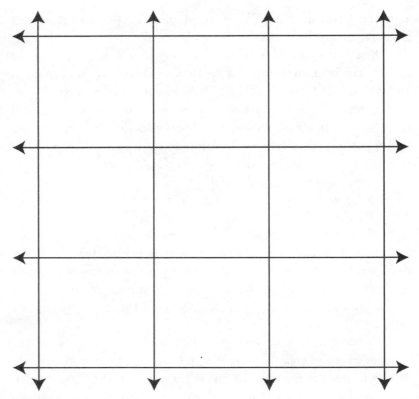

Figure 5-7
By seeding in two directions your coverage will be much better.

best because there are several types and or varieties of seed present. Each seed type is more likely to find a suitable location to grow in. Look for at least a middle of the line quality of seed if price is the only thing you are concerned with or if you are not familiar with grass seeds. You might want to use for example, in the Northern Midwest, a combination of 70 percent bluegrass with a 30 percent ryegrass mixture. The southern parts of the Midwest and transition zone would be more suited for fescue blends. The key is to have varieties mixed together that will complement one another and help guarantee the success of the seeding project.

The last stage for seeding an area is to apply straw over the newly seeded area. Straw has several functions for a seeding project:

- The first and most important being erosion control. If the seeding project you are working on is on a steep incline or in an area where runoff is a concern then you will probably want to cover the seed a little heavier than normal. This will help to slow runoff and minimize damage from rainfall while the grass is establishing itself.

- The straw will also help to retain any moisture the seeding receives during rains or irrigation. Straw has a hollow porous nature which retains a tremendous amount of moisture. This moisture will then be available for the new grass as it grows.

- The straw shields the soil surface from intense sunlight and protects newly emerging grass plants once they germinate.

- Straw will also help to increase germination times drastically. The reason is due to a canopy effect it creates. The grass seeds germinate and due to the natural phototropic nature of plants the grass shoots up for light. This will make the grass seem to appear magically overnight sometimes because it can happen so quickly.

- Once it is time for the first mowing and the straw is shredded up with a mower, there is the slight benefit of the organic matter added to the soil from the mulched up straw.

There are situations where straw is not needed and there are a couple of disadvantages to using straw. The biggest disadvantage to using straw is from the amount of weeds that you may be introducing back to your newly seeded area. Straw is usually cut from mature

DID YOU KNOW?
The biggest disadvantage to using straw may be the amount of weeds that you may be introducing back to your newly seeded area.

wheat after the seed heads are harvested or sometimes from other agriculture crops like barley. The straw should always be purchased from someone who has a reputation for providing high quality straw from well maintained fields free from noxious weeds.

If there are a few weeds in the straw it is not a long term concern because all turf needs to have a weed treatment program put into effect after establishment. Grass will germinate and grow without straw as long as there is good seed to soil contact. The establishment period will take longer for uncovered grass compared to an area that was covered with straw.

Wind is a factor to consider when applying straw especially if you do not have irrigation or a water source for your seeding project. If you are trying to seed a part of a lawn that is on the top of a hill

FIGURE 5-8
Straw blowers can save you hours of time compared to spreading the straw by hand.

where you cannot get water to it, straw might be a waste of time and money. Wind can blow the straw away before you get any benefit from using it. This is another reason for the use of a mechanical seeder. If the seed is incorporated into the soil the need for straw is not a serious one.

When applying straw most people still "shake out bales" by hand. This is just the old fashioned way of picking up a chunk of straw and shaking it out into smaller pieces when covering the seed. There are now many types of straw application equipment. These "straw blowers" as they are called, have a shredding device in them with a blower that shoots the straw out onto the seeding. Some of the units have long hoses to disperse the straw while others mount on trucks and shoot bales out like they are coming out of a cannon.

There are only certain times of the year when any type seeding should be considered. This will vary somewhat based on the particular seasons in your area as well as the type of grass you are trying to establish. Spring and fall are certainly your best choices for grass establishment. Fall is the best time of the year to try a seeding project because turfgrass will tend to develop better roots in the fall than in spring. When you seed in spring you should be thinking of weed control instead. In the Midwest you should start seeding projects around the first of March and be seeding no later than the first of June. A fall seeding project should be done sometime between the end of August through the beginning of November. This is certainly not an exact schedule of what happens every year due to the variation in seasons from year to year. There could be specific weather issues that could delay or speed up your scheduled time frame.

The reason that spring and fall work best is because rain is more likely and soil temps are the most suitable for seed germination during these time frames. These dates are going to provide the best results for trying to grow cool season grasses. Warm season grasses are usually established by different methods and are done at different times of the year.

There should be some consideration given to weeds when seeding which is why the use of straw is often contemplated. Weeds are usually more of an issue after the grass is up and established. When seeding is performed in late spring there should always be a fear of summer annual weeds, especially crabgrass. This is one of the many reasons why grass should be sown in the fall vs. the spring. Weed treatments while seeding are almost impossible because chemicals will directly affect seed germination. A good rule of thumb when seeding should be to wait four to six weeks or after two mowings before any chemical treatments are put down. This is especially true for broadleaf herbicides which tend to be the most harmful to young grass plants. There is a chemical that is known as Tupersan that can be used while seeding in late spring and is often found on many starter fertilizers. Tupersan is the generic name for one of the few known grass herbicides that can be used while seeding. It is primarily used as a crabgrass preventative and is fairly effective when used this way. Most other common chemicals that are used on turf should be avoided until the new grass has had time to grow.

Once a seeding project has been completed, the first thing to think about is water, regardless if any fertilizers and/or chemicals were used. All seeds need water to germinate and continue a healthy level of growth. Remember that water is the main component of grass and it does not grow very well without it. A new seeding ideally would receive $1/10"$ to $2/10"$ of moisture per day for at least the first couple of weeks. Most grasses germinate in 14–21 days or less and moisture is important to the germination process. Watering regularly insures a successful start to lawn establishment and you should continue to give the seeding a $1/4$ inch of moisture every other day for four to six weeks. If you do not have an irrigation system then watering can be done with a garden hose, a sprinkler or by many other methods. The idea is that the grass should receive a nice steady rate of moisture over a long period of time vs. a deluge of water for just a few minutes. This will help to minimize runoff and erosion while allowing the grass to grow. By watering lightly for longer periods of time the water will have time to soak down to the roots. A project that is covered with straw

---

PRO POINTER

A project that is covered with straw should be watered in as quickly after completion as possible to get the straw saturated so it will retain moisture and not blow away.

should be watered as quickly after completion as possible to get the straw saturated so it will retain moisture and not blow away.

There is a specialized machine that is now being used for seeding projects that you need to be aware of. Devices know as hydro-seeders are now becoming more popular than ever. The problem with hydro-seeding is it often creates an attractive lawn for the short term. The concept of a hydro-seeder is that a mulching component is mixed into a large water tank along with fertilizer and all of the "elements necessary for a beautiful lawn." This type of machine may not be the best and most effective way to create a lawn. There is always an inconsistency in the result of the seeding because everything that is mixed in the tank is of different sizes and textures. Also there is no chance for incorporation of elements into the soil unless this is done prior to using the machine. A hydro-seeder can provide an excellent stand of turf but it often is short lived because of the lack of soil improvement that is usually done. In most cases these machines are used right after construction and they tend to just cover up hard nasty soils with a colored mulch with a little grass in it. Hydro-seeding is a valuable tool for seeding highway projects or medians because these machines can cover large areas of ground without ever having to drive over the top of the surface at all but the normal seeding process will be much better suited for your lawn.

Any lawn you have established should be able to be mowed within a few weeks of establishment. Do not believe the old wives tale that grass should seed out before the first mowing. That is simply no where close to the reality of what should occur. Mowing should start when the majority of the seedling grass has reached a height that normal mowing might occur at or just slightly higher than that. Mow around four to five inches in height at first and cut the grass no lower than two and one half inch to three inches when mowing after that. A two and one half inch to three inch mowing height for cool season grasses will not be create a shock to the new seedling grass. Mowing is very important at the establishment stage to cause the grass to tiller and spread. Once a grass plant is mowed it begins to explore new avenues of spreading out on its own. Be cautious not to mow the ground if it is too wet the first time. You may have spent a lot of time on your project and you do not want to mess it up with ruts from a heavy mower.

Controlling weeds while establishing grass can be difficult if not impossible but there should be a weed control program put into effect as quickly after establishment as possible. A good weed and fertility program is well worth it when compared to repeated costs of renovation or replacement. A well maintained lawn will last for years if all treatments are done in a correct timeframe and the other maintenance is kept up. If the weather gets dry then it is time to get out the sprinklers. Retest the ph of the lawn on a minimum of every three years and make sure that those weeds are kept under control. Do not be one of those homeowners who lets a newly established lawn turn into a mess within the first year or two because there is no control of the weeds. Establishment is half of the game, the other half is keeping it looking that way. Invasive weeds only need a short window to come into a lawn and ruin its appearance.

6

Creating Lawn From Sod

The fastest and most effective way to establish grass in a short period of time is through the process of sodding. If your project is one of urgency then there is no faster way to create a beautiful looking lawn. Sodding is the process of laying carpet-like pieces of turfgrass over the top of the soil to create "instant grass." The sod that is used will have been harvested from a sod farm. These pieces of sod are cut with specialized pieces of equipment called sod cutters. The sod may range from one-half to two inches in thickness and often comes in three to nine foot lengths for easy handling. The pieces of sod are arranged to cover up a dirt area just as you would lay carpet on a floor, eventually creating the perfect instant lawn.

SOD

Sod can be bought in large rolls but these require additional specialized equipment to then lay the sod. Large rolls are seldom used in lawns but are commonly used for athletic fields or large scale projects. Sod is used for immediate effect for the most part and there are many circumstances that can create the need for an instant yard. Many contractors and landscape professionals find that sod is very good for providing the instant finished look that many people will pay lots of money to have. Sod also eliminates the concerns for immediate weed control, however, it does not eliminate the need for water.

Some of the reasons sod might be used instead of seeding:

- Provide an instant finished look
- Eliminate the mess a seeding project creates
- Create a quick fix for erosion concerns
- Take care of an immediate need for a lawn for a special event
- Provide a playing surface for athletes

FIGURE 6-1
Newly-laid sod on this golf course tee provides an immediate playing surface instead of having to wait for seedling grass to grow.

When you purchase sod it will arrive with a certain amount of soil attached to the base of the root zone area. Essentially you are buying a layer of grass with some soil still attached to it. When you

PRO POINTER
Consider the source of the sod and that the field may potentially have assessed for weed problems or a lack of fertility.

purchase your sod you often may not know a lot about the location or history of the soil where this sod came from. Consider the source of the sod and that, potentially, that field may have possessed weed problems or a lack of fertility. You are only getting the top one-half to one inch of soil when you purchase sod but you may not have a lot of information about the soil that the sod was grown in. Typically sod may have been harvested off of the farm for years which can be both good and bad. The good news is it will be easy for you to check with others in your area that may have purchased sod from the same supplier to see if they experienced an unusual weed or fertility problem in years following the sod installation. The bad news is that sod is harvested year after year from the same fields and that over time there is less top soil and more sub soil being harvested each time the fields are cut. This could create a continual decline in the quality of the sod and soil you are buying if the sod farmer is not properly taking care of the sod fields from year to year. In some cases the top-soil attached to the sod is low in nutrients and it could also be at an undesirable ph because it has been stripped out of the same fields for so long without anything added back to it. This is why there should still be some consideration for site preparation even before sod is laid. The following is a list of the basic steps for sod installation:

1. Evaluate the existing soil and soil test the soil that is there.

2. Investigate the sod farm source and the quality of that sod.

3. Measure your site and calculate the yards needed and cost of the sod.

4. Incorporate materials such as organic matter, pelletized lime, or fertilizer to improve the soil with a tilling process. Try to shallow till if possible.

5. Use a roller to level out the tilled area. Keep in mind small bumps will make sod installation very difficult.

6. Make sure that the grade is very smooth to eliminate bumps and humps that will show up under the sod after it is put in

7. Lay the sod over the desired areas. Be sure to pull seams close together.

8. Spread soil in any large voids between pieces to additionally level out the lawn.

9. Irrigate the area to insure a successful stand.

Ideally the same things are looked at by someone laying sod as would be by a person preparing for a seeding job. The soil is the most critical area to improve to insure the long term success of the sod laying project. This means that tilling may still be needed to incorporate all of the proper elements into the soil prior to laying the sod out. If tilling is done you must make sure that the area is raked or rolled out very smooth prior to the actual installation of the sod. It would be like trying to roll a carpet out over a floor covered with golf balls and baseballs. By doing the proper site prep problems of uneven turf can be eliminated later on. Although sod is fairly easy to install, it can be a tedious process.

The process of laying sod can be done without a professionals help but you have to do things right the first time and there is little margin for error. Sod will most often come in rolled pieces that are 1 ½' wide and nine feet in length. The first thing to do when planning to install sod is to calculate how much sod you will need and what exactly this sod will cost.

For example, figure the distance in feet of the area you want to cover with your lawn. Fifty feet by 100 feet would be 5,000 square feet. Divide 5,000 by nine to convert your figure into square yards

You should order approximately 556 yards of sod for your project. Order some extra for mistakes or where many pieces will need to cut. Find out your cost per yard to purchase sod and multiply it by the number of yards you think you will need. In this case it might be 556 yards @ $1.50 per yard.

Calculating your cost is an important step to deciding if you can even afford to install sod. Sod is very expensive and you should be cautious in every step of the process to make sure you get things right the first time. If your sod is not installed properly or if it

is not taken care of, the costs for failure could be quite high. The average market cost for sod will vary by geographic location so it would be hard to say what you could expect to pay for sod in your area.

Sod needs to be installed starting from one corner point. It is easier if your starting point is a square corner but that is not always possible in odd shaped lawns. The sod should be installed so the strips are laid as closely together as possible. You should use your hands or a rake to pull the pieces as tightly together as you can get them. Eliminating seams is the difference from your sod looking good or bad when you are finished. If you have obstacles to work around you can use a spade to cut the sod in pieces to work around obstacles. You will need to fill in voids if there are curves or areas where you cannot get the seams perfect. I would suggest taking a mixture of soil with peat moss mixed in it and filling in the open voids between the pieces. Spread a little seed on the fill dirt you put into the seams if they are large. Be sure to use a grass seed type consistent with the sod that you purchased.

Make sure that you are leveling the ground as much as possible as you are laying the sod. Any slightly uneven area or bump under the sod will be hard to take care of after the ground is covered up. This may seem like a tedious process but the more careful you are the better off your results will be.

Probably the biggest requirement of sod is the large amount of water it will need for a few weeks after being installed. Sod has a reaction of shock for a time period after installation. The first few weeks after sod is laid it is trying to find a source ofr water and to grow roots. Since its roots were severed in the sod field when it was har-

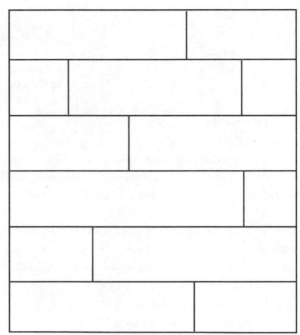

Figure 6-2
This drawing would be the typical pattern for laying sod. Notice how the seams are staggered.

vested it takes time to establish a good basis to where it can start taking up water again. You should give sod ¼ inch of water or more a day for two to four weeks or until established. You should always install your sod in the spring or the fall because of the generous rains you are likely to receive.

Sod should be mowed at about the same height you would normally mow grass and you will want to mow as soon as conditions allow for it. Just like a seeding project you will want to mow a little higher than normal at first to eliminate stress to the turf. Sod usually takes a while before the grass tips grow tall enough to be mowed. It takes a while for the sod to root well enough to establish top growth. Once the sod roots itself then top growth seems to happen very quickly. Make sure the subsoil is not too wet to put mowing

> **TECH TIP**
> You should give sod 1/4 inch of water or more a day for 2 to 4 weeks or until established.

equipment onto the sod that could cause damage to the grass plants. It is easy to scalp the new sod if the ground is uneven and recovery is very slow and unsightly if that happens. Be patient with the establishment process and understand that even though the sod may look good it still takes time before you truly have a lawn you can play on.

Sod can be laid right over the top of existing grass or undisturbed ground. This will provide a fairly level surface for installation of the sod, but this may not be the most ideal conditions for rooting. It you have laid the sod out without doing any soil improvements make sure that a light application of a starter fertilizer is applied over the top when you are finished. You should always use a soil test for the basis of any type of soil improvements. Fertilizers high in nitrogen content are not necessary because ideally you are trying to establish roots and not top growth at this point. I would always recommend improving the soil if you can but sometimes it is easier to lay sod over the top of the existing lawn.

ESTABLISHMENT OF WARM SEASON GRASSES

With warm season grasses the methods for establishment are quite different than most cool season grasses. In most cases seeding is not an option for establishment which makes sodding the only choice for establishment if you want to have a warm season lawn. Sodding is done for any large scale warm season grass establishment just the same as it would be for any cool season grasses. Warm season grass sod farms are not that common through most of the transition zone so you can expect to pay a premium for the sod you purchase. In the south warm season grass is much more common and most sod farms will offer a couple of choices for warm season grass.

PLUGGING

One way to establish warm season grasses on a smaller scale is through a method referred to as plugging. Plugging is probably more commonly known when used for establishment of Zoysia grass. Zoysia, like many other warm season grasses, is only available in sod or plugs and they can not be seeded. Plugging, in this case, is different than the references made to core aerating. Plugging is done through the use a hand tool that is actually called a plugger. This tool for simplified descriptions is a hollow tube that has a handle of some sort on the end. The idea is to drive two to three inches into the soil surface to pull a core that can be transplanted into a new location. Cool season grasses can also be plugged, but this process is much more common to establishment of warm season grass.

It is possible to convert your cool season grass to warm season grass through the process of plugging. When plugging for replacement of cool season grass a plug of cool season grass is pulled out and a new one of warm season is put back in. Warm season grasses tend to be much more aggressive than cool season turf so eventually they will take over the cool season turf. It is nearly impossible to convert warm season turf to cool season grass using a plugging process. Warm season grasses would need to be killed out or removed completely for any hopes of converting warm to cool season grass this way.

Plugging can be useful for more than establishment though. Golf course professionals have used plugging to repair damaged areas on greens and tees for years. In this case the damaged area is removed and the plug of healthy new grass is put back in. When plugging warm season grasses you should do the plugging when the grass is actively growing if possible. You can establish plugs when grass is dormant also. Keep in mind dormant plugs will root just fine once temperatures reach a point desirable for

DID YOU KNOW?

Warm season grasses tend to be much more aggressive than cool season turf so eventually they will take over the cool season turf.

FIGURE 6-3
Typical plugging device.

growth of the plants. Plugging is a crude and simple process, but this is the cheapest and most effective way to establish many warm season grasses. Sodding will provide much faster results but plugging will look the same after several years. Plugs are certainly much cheaper than sodding an area and probably why they are so popular. It requires little skill or knowledge of turf to do plugging and Zoysia grass is marketed in popular gardening magazines for that very reason. The ads might read "buy 20 plugs receive a plugger for free" which is why plugging became so popular for Zoysia establishment. It was this marketing approach that moved warm season grasses far into the transition zone and areas to the North.

These are some types of warm season grasses that can be plugged:

- Zoysia
- Bermuda
- St. Augustine

SPRIGGING

Another way to establish warm season grasses is through a process of sprigging. Sprigging is commonly used for larger scale projects more specifically for the use on golf course fairways. Many golf courses in the Midwest in recent years have made a transition to the warm season Zoysia grass or Bermuda grass. This has been done due to the demand from golfers for higher playing standards. The warm season grasses can be maintained at much lower heights and have other more desirable characteristics for golfing as well. You could potentially use this process for a large area warm season lawn installation so you should be aware of what it is. The sprigging process consists of is using small pieces of tillers and rhizomes and simply broadcasting them out over an area and heavily watering them in. It is kind of like spreading shreds of actively growing turf over the top of other turf and watching them take over. The reason this method is used is, once again, cost. This is an effective method for establishment even though it may seem like an odd approach to grass establishment.

CONCLUSION

These are the most common methods for sod establishment. There are ways to establish warm season grasses by seed, as well as ways to plug and sprig cool season grasses but for the most part the methods that are done stay the same. There are arguably advantages and disadvantages to all seeding and sodding methods. It is up to you to assess each circumstance to determine which ones will work best for you.

7

Watering and Erosion

S ince grass is composed primarily of water it only makes sense that watering is an important part of the care of your lawn. Watering seems like it would be a straight forward process that cannot be done incorrectly, but like anything—more is not always better. Watering should be approached with the understanding that too much water can be just as harmful as not enough water.

WATERING EQUIPMENT

The process of watering the lawn does not require an irrigation system to correctly maintain the condition of your lawn. Lawns can be kept just as lush and beautiful with a garden hose and sprinkler compared to lawns with full scale irrigation systems. In fact most lawns in the United States do not have full scale irrigation systems in them. Technology is increasing the numbers of lawns that are irrigated every day but most people rely on some type of nozzle hooked to the end of the garden hose to take care of their watering needs. It is the process of watering and how you do it that will provide your success and not necessarily the device you have to do your watering with.

A hose and sprinkler system is readily available and it is something that is practically affordable by anyone. The use of the water may not be affordable to do over long periods of time but the cost of the device itself is very inexpensive. You can successfully water a lawn and have a perfect looking lawn without the use of expensive irrigation systems. Irrigation is very handy and you could expect to spend a lot of time with a garden hose trying to get the same result. If you are looking to minimize the effort of watering then irrigation will be

FIGURE 7-1
A sprinkler on a garden hose may seem like a simple device. However, the device you are using to water is not as important as the manner in which you water.

must. Also if your lawn is large then a garden hose will be impractical and covering the whole lawn will be nearly impossible if dry conditions persist for long periods of time.

EFFECTIVE WATERING TECHNIQUES

One of the keys to watering is really not to water the grass but rather to water the soil. The grass takes moisture up from the soil through the root zone so this is where your focus needs to be. Even though the soil may appear dry to the naked eye, the grass plants are able to utilize moisture in the soil. The key to watering is: Water only when necessary. It is true that once you "train" grass to expect daily watering, the grass will then show drought stress even more quickly than normal. Many people feel a need to run an irrigation system daily even if they do not really need to water. This need sometimes comes from the cost associated with the irrigation, but you do not need to irrigate every day. Watering everyday when it is not needed will only create a turf that is not healthy and is dependant on water. These are a few things that can occur from over watering:

- Turf may appear stressed very quickly when water is not available.
- The grass could be more susceptible to disease.
- Roots can become unhealthy and not able to search for their own water.
- Water can pool on the soil surface and actually kill areas of grass.
- Soils that are saturated can be easily damaged by mowers or foot traffic.
- Compaction is more likely with saturated soils.
- Water runoff can create problems with pollution and erosion.

The following is a list of things that can affect the water needs of turfgrass:

- Weather patterns
- Cloud cover
- Rainfall
- Wind
- Air temperature
- Turf conditions/ Turf stress
- Time of the year- Hours of sunlight/Length of the day
- Humidity
- Soil temperature
- Slope and grade of the yard
- Evaporation

Any one of these things or a combination of things can have a direct effect on the amount of water you need to apply to the lawn. It is hard to interpret the effect of these factors but each one will vary the water your turfgrass will require.

DETERMINING THE AMOUNT OF WATER NEEDED

Not all grass types need the same amount of water. Some grasses such as Bluegrass are more glutinous in their water consumption compared to Fescue or Bermuda grass. The water needs of turfgrass can vary based on the stage of development that they are in. Seedling grass has a much more immediate and constant need for water compared to mature turfgrass that has an established root zone. Since young turfgrass does not have a developed root system it is unable to search out and find an adequate water supply. You should assume

DID YOU KNOW?
The water needs of turfgrass can also vary based on its stage of development.

that if you are not able to provide water to young turfgrass that much of the grass will die after germination and be replaced with weeds instead.

There are no textbook rules for exactly how much water you should give your lawn. Most lawns require a 1/10 inch of water per day or a ¼ inch of moisture every two to three days (these are only averages and the numbers can vary). It may be better for established lawns to be watered less frequently, but deeply, instead of watering everyday. If you are watering a new seedling stand then it would be more advantageous to use ¹/₁₀ inch of water a day. Water needs could be much higher during hot and dry conditions where you would be forced to use ¼ inch of water a day just to sustain a nice healthy green look. Keep in mind that once you start to water on a regular basis it will be hard to stop without seeing stress in the turf. You should be cautious on using a "certain" amount of water due to all of the variables with watering.

BENEFITS OF WEATHER EVENTS

Never give up on the benefits of Mother Nature compared to supplemental water you are providing to keep your lawn looking healthy. There are no substitutes to the benefits of rain water compared to using city water. Fluoride and chlorine are found in city water and both of these can affect plants in negative ways. If you are using a city water source you are putting things into the lawn that you may not be aware are in the water. Lake and well water are typically better for your lawn than city water but rain is still the best. Unless you are in a region prone to acid rain or high pollution, rain water provides the cleanest and best source of water for any lawn, and a good thunderstorm adds even another benefit. Lighting is the only phenomena in nature that fixes nitrogen in the soil and makes that nitrogen plant available. This is one of the reasons a "good old thunderstorm" tends to green up the lawn quickly compared to the frequent watering you are giving with a supplemental water source such as irrigation.

FIGURE 7-2
Lightning storm.

WATERING SCHEDULE

Watering time is as critical to your success as the amount of water you are applying to the turfgrass. You should always try to water your grass in the early morning right before or after the sun rises. This time will vary based on the time of the year and day length but the method should remain the same. There is an old saying that "you should never put a lawn to bed wet." There are several reasons why you should water early in the morning:

- Watering during extreme heat can cause leaf scorch during hot and dry conditions.

- Water can increase the causes for disease and help to spread disease if the grass leaves are not able to dry off.

- Wet turfgrass plants can develop an unhealthy condition or root problems when not allowed to dry properly.

- You are less likely to have interference with people and pets when watering early in the day.

IRRIGATION SYSTEMS

Watering with an irrigation system allows you to set a timer that can easily allow watering at the appropriate times. An irrigation system can run its cycle and not need a human intervention on a daily basis. Watering the lawn "by hand" with a hose and sprinkler will take a long period of time. Since it will take so long you may find that you are not watering during appropriate times. It would be difficult or impossible to properly water a large lawn with a garden hose and sprinkler during the mornings only. Then you have to weigh the options of watering during the heat of the day and creating more problems compared to not watering at all. A hose and a sprinkler can usually cover a 20 to 30 foot radius and put down a $1/10$ inch of moisture in 10 to 15 minutes under normal water pressure. This means that you could easily cover a 5,000 square foot lawn in a couple of hours if you have the time to do it. Watering successfully without

PRO POINTER
Syringing the grass is a process in which you turn on the irrigation system or sprinkler for just a few revolutions of the sprinkler heads.

irrigation can easily be done but it does take a lot of extra work, and time to get the same results.

There are times when watering during the heat of the day can benefit the lawn. Syringing the grass is when you turn on the irrigation system or sprinkler for just a few revolutions of the sprinkler heads. This process helps to cool off heat stressed grass leaves and air temperatures in seconds.

Evaporation is a possible problem that can require you to water more than normal. Evaporation during a normal watering will not allow all of the water you are applying to actually reach the ground. The rate of evaporation and water loss will be higher as temperatures increase. Wind and humidity can also have an effect on the amount

FIGURE 7-3
It takes only a short period of time for runoff water to create huge erosion problems both on and off of the property you are trying to water, as evidenced in this photo.

evaporation that is occurring. If you are experiencing a lot of evaporation during the course of your watering you may have to increase the amount of time you water in order to get the same result.

RUNOFF AND EROSION

Although the water you are applying to the lawn is intended for the grass not all of the water has time to be absorbed right away. Water runoff is a huge concern for many reasons.

This is a list of what damage runoff water can cause:

- Pollutants such as fertilizer and pesticide residues can be carried into water sources like lakes and streams.

- Heavy runoff can create huge erosion problems that carry away valuable topsoil.

FIGURE 7-4
Since lawns usually run right up to street edges, the water that comes off lawns ends up in storm drains or sewers.

- Runoff water can end up in low lying areas where it can stagnate and harbor insects and disease.

- Water is a limited resource and any runoff should be considered a waste of that resource.

Dealing with your runoff is an important part of the watering process. Make sure that all of your sprinklers are covering the area that you are intending to water. Over watering will create runoff water which will lead to larger problems.

The following is a list of things you can do to reduce runoff water:

- Eliminate bare areas of soil in or around the lawn so vegetation will absorb the water.

- If you have a large piece of property, you can create drainage systems that direct water to run a certain way which will eliminate runoff.

- Avoid over watering the lawn whenever possible.

- Plant shrubs and trees in low lying areas where water is likely to pool or stand.

CONCLUSION

It is nearly impossible to eliminate runoff water completely if you choose to water your lawn. As long as you use some common sense strategies and stay aware of the negative effects of runoff, you can safely and successfully have the perfect lawn.

8

Lawn Fertilization

When you are thinking about your lawn and dream about what the perfect lawn will look like, you probably would use the word "green" in your description. It could be said that anyone who wants a dark green lawn would have to use some sort of fertilizer to get the greenest color in your lawn. The key to a green lawn is through the use of fertilizer but you should never use fertilizer for the sole purpose of trying to get a dark green color.

FERTILIZER FUNCTIONS

Fertilizer serves several functions that will give you the ideal-looking yard and a dark green color which is just an added benefit. Following is a list of the benefits of what fertilizer will do for your turfgrass:

- Provides a deep green color in the lawn
- Adds nutrients to the soil for uptake by turfgrass plants
- Improves turfgrass health overall

- Improves turf density and rigidity
- Enhances rooting of the grass plants

When fertilizer is added to the turf, there is almost always a benefit but there is a certain time and method to a fertilizer application. There are even a few instances when the addition of fertilizers can do more harm than good to the grass when applied at the wrong time. Fertilizer should be used for the intentions of root growth and not for the purpose of top growth. We all wish we had a green healthy lawn but no one wants to mow every two or three days from a misapplication of fertilizer. It is the timing of the application that will give you the result you desire.

Fertilizer is the key to having healthy dark green turf that is free from stress and disease. Fertilizer can come in many different forms which have different release properties that make the fertilizer available for grass at certain times. Each type of fertilizer has a specific analysis that will provide the nutrients you specifically need to add to the lawn. The nutrient needs can be determined through the use of a soil test which you should have done at least every three years. There are types of fertilizers that should be used on turfgrass that are more suited for turfgrass use and you should be aware that all fertilizers are not the same.

FERTILIZER TYPES

Two of the most common types of fertilizers that you will find for use on turf will be either a urea-based fertilizer or an ammonium nitrate-based fertilizer. These fertilizers can possess slow release properties through some chemistry but typically they are a quick release type of fertilizer. These types of fertilizers have been used for many years and are readily available for purchase under numerous brand names or through bulk purchase at a co-op. They are still used today and they are very effective for general use on lawns. Any combina-

---

PRO POINTER

Nutrient needs can be determined through the use of a soil test which you should have done at least every three years.

tion of the elements N-P-K can be found in fertilizers but a micronutrient package is fairly uncommon unless it is a more reputable brand or special blend by request. Urea based fertilizers are very popular in the agriculture industry where they are used in fields and pastures. They are also used on golf courses and in the lawn care for turf applications. The main reason that a quick release urea type fertilizer would be used is because of cost. Quick release urea and ammonium nitrate fertilizers are still some of the cheapest types of fertilizers that can be used. The price of fertilizers are dictated slightly by fuel prices because heat is required to manufacture them so fertilizer prices in general will increase during times when fuel is high.

One type of fertilizer that is a step up from a basic urea fertilizer is an SCU or sulfur coated urea fertilizer. This is a urea based fertilizers but it also has a coating that gives the fertilizer a slow release quality that makes them very desirable. There is not a huge price increase over the traditional counterpart of a standard urea. The combination of SCU is usually mixed in with a regular urea fertilizer giving the total package of fertilizer that is readily available and other that will be slow release. The slow release portion could be expected to last three to six months depending on many other factors:

- Chemistry or technology of the SCU coating

- Amount of rain (rain can leach out fertilizers in the soil)

- Soil microbial activity

- Amount of beneficial organisms in the soil

- Condition and texture of the soil

There are other types of slow release urea and ammonium nitrate fertilizers that use different technologies for the release mechanism. For example there are methylene ureas and other coated urea fertilizers. Each of the different types of slow-release fertilizers range in their effectiveness based on the technology used to create the fertilizer and the desired effect from the use of the fertilizer. There are many types of slow-release fertilizers in existence and the technology is changing very rapidly in how slow-release fertilizers work. The best

TECH TIP
The best fertilizer to be used on turf would need to be some sort of a slow-release fertilizer mixed in with a quick-release fertilizer.

fertilizer to be used on turf would need to be some sort of a slow-release type fertilizer mixed in with a quick-release fertilizer. For instance the product might contain 50% slow release and 50% quick release. This type of product would be ideal, for example, if it was put down in the fall. The quick release will give the grass a quick jump start while the slow-release portion of the product would continue to feed on into the winter.

There are other types of fertilizers that are slow release and are coated with a poly coating or even some sort of plastic like coating. One example of a similar product is called Osmocote™, which is a ammonium nitrate based fertilizer coated with a plastic type of coating which makes it slow release. The beneficial organisms found in the soil, in combination with moisture, work on the coating as the fertilizers and bits of organisms are released a little at a time. These types of coating advertise six to nine months of slow release properties. Extreme heat or extreme freezing temperatures can cause some coatings to break down prematurely causing a more immediate dump of the Nitrogen than is desired. Consider your timing of the application because this could be a concern.

FERTILIZER APPLICATION

When you consider the differences in quick release fertilizers versus a slow release fertilizer many people choose not to use slow release fertilizer due to the cost. You need to be aware that for example a quick release fertilizer could have a leaching rate that would cause a five times multiplier to the amount of the fertilizer needed to match the amount that is utilized in a slow release type of fertilizer. When you consider that you are really not saving any money at all because much of the fertilizer is lost and never available to the plants. Not only is that not good for the pocket book but it is also bad for the environment because fertilizers pollute our water sources. Fertilizer run off is a growing concern to environment and many companies

FIGURE 8-1
Osmocote ™ offers a 120-day release. This is a coated ammonium nitrate fertilizer.

are changing technology and analysis of fertilizers to help out the environment.

All granular fertilizers come in small particle form and are dry for easy spreading with drop or rotary spreaders. You should use a rotary spreader for applying fertilizer vs. using a drop spreader if you can. Rotary spreaders insure a more even distribution and leave less chance for overlap and turf burning compared to a drop spreader. Another way to help improve distribution and consistency is by using fertilizers that are well blended and have consistent particle sizes that spread easily. There are several types of fertilizer blends that are used when it comes to brands of fertilizer. Some companies use what are called homogenous blended fertilizers. Homogenous blends insure product consistency and more evenly sized fertilizer particles. The idea is that the fertilizer will spread more consistently and evenly. This will help to make sure that all of the turfgrass areas you are spreading the product on receive even coverage and consistent amounts of each element.

FIGURE 8-2
Using a rotary-type spreader to apply fertilizer to the lawn.

There are really many technologies and features of fertilizers that make each one unique. The purpose of fertilizer is to enhance turf quality, be available when needed, and provide a well balanced release mechanism. Some fertilizers are immediately available and provide the plant with an instant jump start where others provide long term feeding to the turfgrass. Fertilizers are available in forms other than granular. A very popular choice for fertilizer application by lawn care companies is to use liquid fertilization. This is a common way for lawn care operations to be able to supplement fertilizer needs to the lawn along with a weed treatment at the same time. The practice of liquid fertilizing is done by lawn care companies to give lawns a quick burst of green color or to rejuvenate the grass along with a weed treatment. Liquid fertilizers usually only provide a short term effect and you should not use a liquid fertilizer for the entire growing season for you lawn care needs.

Liquid fertilizer provides an immediate but temporary availability to turfgrass plants. The problem with liquid fertilizing is once the plant has used up this liquid form of Nitrogen that was applied, there is little else available for the turfgrass consumption. Liquids move quickly through the plant and they do give it an instant burst of green color. However, liquid fertilizers often are being applied to turfgrass plants at times and at rates that are not conducive for fertilizer treatments. There are many lawn care companies that claim to offer slow release liquid fertilizers which do have slow release qualities. There is no comparison of a liquid fertilizer for long term feeding compared to the results provided by high quality coated fertilizers.

> **DID YOU KNOW?**
> A very popular choice of lawn care companies for fertilizer application is liquid fertilization. This is a common way for lawn care operations to be able to supplement the lawn's fertilizer needs with a weed treatment at the same time.

ALTERNATIVE FERTILIZERS

Fertilizer and pesticide problems in our environment raise more concerns in consumer's minds than ever before. Problems associated with fertilizer and chemicals are more common than they were in years past. Organic gardening and alternative lawn care has created a great demand for manure or organic based fertilizer. These fertilizers are made from things such as recycled human and pet waste, fish and plant byproducts, or composted and recycled materials. The whole idea is to create a totally organic product that is still easy to spread. Some fertilizers offer a valued natural side effect of disease resistance and color enhancement. Turfgrass responds very well to the organics but typically availability and price has limited their usage. Anything new or difficult to produce comes with a price tag. As the demand continues for more environmentally friendly products, prices have fallen and newer improved products are being created. There are products that are available that use things like chicken manure or other composted materials. Some products have an odor or spread ability concern but you could expect tremendous period of dark green color, disease resistance, and improved turf quality.

FERTILIZING TECHNIQUES

The use of fertilizer is a necessary practice associated with turfgrass growth and production. In most cases the existing soil that is being utilized for grass establishment is going to be deficient in some or all of the elements required to keep turf looking its best. Turfgrass prefers to have an abundance of Nitrogen, Phosphorus, and Potassium available for growth. Turfgrass also has a need for several minor elements as well. Proper fertilization and soil fertility is the key to turfgrass success.

Grass has a specific time frame that fertilizer should be applied in and it is different for warm season and cool season grasses. The biggest problem with many home owners or private individuals doing their own yard is to fertilize at the wrong time of the year. Part of the problem has come about from the marketing practices of retailers and manufactures who sell fertilizers and lawn care products. By the time you as an individual are seeing fertilizers on the shelf, half of the application time frame has passed in many cases. When using fertilizer the key to good fertilizing methods is to promote root growth and not top growth.

There is a general calculation of fertilizer the figures the fertilizer in amount in pounds of Nitrogen per 1,000 square feet. The amount of Nitrogen is calculated based on the analysis of the fertilizer and then figuring out exactly how much of the product is used to provide a pound of Nitrogen per 1,000 square foot of ground covered. Most labels will give you estimations of how many pounds of the total bag of fertilizer will need to be applied to get the desired result of pounds per 1,000. Phosphorus and Potassium contents are also important to the total package of the fertilizer applied but since Nitrogen is the most utilized element in fertilizer it is the one usually referred to.

Start with the cool season grasses and the times in which they should be fertilized. It is very common to see fertilizer in the store around late April, May, and even into June. This is great if you are fertilizing warm season turf but not so good for cool season grass. Start with a calendar year by looking at fall first and work toward the summer because this is how your thought process should work when thinking about fertilization. The best time to apply fertilizer is in early fall which in the Midwest is sometime around the first of September and on into late October. At this time, ideally, you would apply one to two pounds of Nitrogen per 1,000 square feet in the form of a slow release fertilizer. You ideally would apply one application to the lawn in September of one pound of Nitrogen per 1,000 square feet and a second application applied in late October or early November of ½ to one pound of Nitrogen per 1,000 square feet. You can apply up to three pounds of Nitrogen per 1,000 square feet in one application, but anything over that amount is almost always a disaster for turf injury. Even two to three pounds per 1,000 square feet can result in turf injury or burning if the application is done incorrectly, especially if it is applied on a hot day. The reason fall is the best time of the year to fertilize is because you are promoting root growth through the entire winter months instead of top growth. It is a given that in the spring all grass will green up, grow like crazy, and is often hard to keep up with when mowing. Then if someone applies too much fertilizer in the spring the lawn can really get out of control. It is unfortunate that retailers have created a perception that spring is best time to fertilizer.

As the winter progresses and the grass goes dormant there is a lot going on in the turfgrass plant that people do not see. Even though the grass on the surface of the soil is brown and dormant for the winter the grass is still very actively growing under the soil. This can be seen by digging into the sod with a knife. You will still see white roots which actively grow and develop under the soil all through the winter months. The grass will utilize the Nitrogen that has been applied to the soil, for the most part, by late winter or early spring. If you are only going to fertilize once a year, fall is the time to do it. However if you are going to fertilize more than once a year then you will want to start thinking about it very early in the spring like late February or March.

If you are going to fertilize in the spring, do it when grass is still partially dormant or just starting to green up. This will "kick start" the grass for the spring growing season and it will still allow some positive root growth early in the year. Grass that has a good root system is able to survive disease and drought much better than grass without a good root system. Roots are the key to good turfgrass growth and without good roots, grass will never appear healthy. If you apply one pound of Nitrogen per 1,000 square feet around the first of March you have met most of the grasses fertilizer needs for the season. You can follow up the spring fertilizing with a light fertilizing sometime in May. This fertilizer application may be accompanied with a weed treatment or even a grub control but the idea is to insure that the grass has that last burst of energy to get through the hot summer months. All of the fertilizer you apply should have some slow release characteristics to insure that something is available for the turfgrass to quickly rejuvenate after it rains.

THE PROBLEM WITH LATE SPRING FERTILIZATION

The problem with fertilizing in the late spring is that the grass is already growing and probably at a very fast rate. If you fertilize late in the spring or summer the grass is only encouraged to grow more. What you are doing is encouraging top growth at the expense of the root system and therefore weakening the plants long term survival capabilities. This is especially true for grass that may not have received any fertilizer in the fall. The plants then shoot out a burst of growth and often bake from hot summer temperatures as the growing season progresses. If the grass plants have no root systems the grass is very slow to recover from the heat or drought stress. Also disease is much more likely to damage turfgrass with no root system.

One misconception of fertilizing in general is that it causes you to mow more often. Properly fertilized turf with an established root system will grow just as slow or slower than turf that has not been fertilized at all. The reason is because the plant is developing and growing in ways that benefit the turf quality instead of just creating shoot growth.

FERTILIZATION OF COOL SEASON TURF

Plants can and will utilize liquid fertilizers in the summer if they are applied in light amounts. They can be effective if the plants have a well developed root system from fall fertilization practices. A little bit of fertilizer is ok to use in mid summer if you have the ability, but a lot of fertilizer does nothing more than cause high stress and turf injury. I do not suggest fertilizing cool season grasses in the Midwest for any reason from the first of June until late August, unless it is with low amounts of Nitrogen in a liquid fertilizer. Low Nitrogen content is essential for doing this type of fertilizing at all.

Ideally turfgrass would prefer to have small "spoon feedings" of Nitrogen through a majority of the year and not a bunch at any one time. Since this is not practical, you should use slow release fertilizers in a good fertilizer program to give basically the same effect. Following is a fertilizer schedule for a one-year season in transition zone:

- February–March: One pound of Nitrogen per 1,000 square feet in 50% or less slow release form can be applied last two weeks in Feb–March. Possibly 28-3-10 (10-50% SCU). Can be used as a carrier for a pre-emergent treatment.

- May–June: ½ pound or less of Nitrogen per 1,000 square feet, slow release is not a necessity. Possibly 12-2-10. This could be a carrier for a post-emergent treatment for crabgrass or other annual weeds. Also could be a carrier for a grub control if one is needed.

- June–August: Supplement liquid fertilizer if used for your program. Low Nitrogen and high water volume would be best. Maybe only use one treatment in combination with weed or late grub treatment, otherwise avoid all together. Try to use no dry fertilizer from June 1 until late August and always very low Nitrogen.

- September: 1.5 pounds of Nitrogen per 1,000 square feet in a slow release fertilizer with 50% SCU or higher. Use 1–1.5 pounds of Nitrogen now and the other in second treatment in October. Possibly a 34-10-18 (50% SCU).

- October–November: One pound of Nitrogen per 1,000 square feet. Use as second fall treatment if 1.5 pounds or less of Nitrogen was applied in early September. Possibly a 20% or less SCU.

This a just one example of a recommended program for cool season turf in the most of the Midwest. Each region can be different and certainly the monthly temps can vary from state to state. This may not be the best program for your area. This program also discourages the use of liquid fertilization.

WARM SEASON FERTILIZATION

Warm season grasses have a different time table that needs to be followed. The concept is quite different from that of cool season grasses. This is especially true for warm season turf grown in the transition zone due to the long periods of dormancy that most warm season grasses have.

The most critical fertilizer applications for warm season grasses are right before and during the actively growing periods in the summer months. I suggest a treatment in late April or early May of one to two pounds of Nitrogen per 1,000 square feet. This will give the grass a good start after a long period of dormancy. This would be the most important treatment to warm season grasses. There can then be follow up treatments of fertilizer at ½-1 pound of Nitrogen in June and again in August.

Warm season grasses like a high amount of Nitrogen available and plenty of moisture while they are actively growing. Then in the winter months while dormant there is little growth activity that occurs. You are not going to notice a patch of Zoysia spreading out or growing in December but rather in July when many of the cool season grasses have gone dormant from the heat. Warm season grasses prefer warm temperatures and an abundance of food and water while they are growing.

9

Mowing and Maintenance

Achieving the perfect lawn is an ongoing process where you must use maintenance as the key for long term success. The most regular form of maintenance you will ever perform on your lawn is the task of mowing. You must balance your lawn maintenance along with environmental conditions like a well scripted play where each variable takes effect at precisely the right moment. If anything is forgotten about for a period of time, or dismissed with no regard for a period of time, then all of the hard work you have put into the yard can be lost for the season. It takes only an incorrect mowing or two to ruin what could have taken literally a couple of years to achieve.

It is possible that skipping critical maintenance, such as a weed treatment application, could create negative effects in the lawn for a whole calendar year. One of the biggest mistakes that people make when considering lawn

DID YOU KNOW?
It takes only an incorrect mowing or two to ruin what could have taken literally a couple of years to achieve.

maintenance is the role of maintenance in general. Achieving the perfect lawn is a difficult task but maintenance is the only way to keep a lawn in the condition you desire on a permanent basis. Mowing must be done at correct intervals and all lawn treatments are sequentially important throughout the growing season. Realize that there is a routine of maintenance that has to be performed in order to keep a lawn in the best shape at all times. Also consider that even with the most perfect maintenance schedules that environmental conditions can still create unforeseen problems. An example, for instance, could be the negative effect of a month of torrential rains or the opposite which could be a sustained drought. Both situations could cancel out a very successful growing season by keeping you from doing the maintenance that is needed.

Mowing would seem like a task that could not be done incorrectly but you can easily make a mistake that could be detrimental to the lawn for the whole season. The equipment you use is the first key to success when addressing the task of mowing. You should look for a mower that has features that will help you in the mowing process. Mowers will not guarantee your success, but a good mower will help to make mowing less of a chore. These are some features a quality mower will possess:

- Cut quality
- Serviceability
- Affordability or cost
- Dependability
- Ease of operation

A good mower will help you with the process of mowing, but you can make mistakes with even the best mowers on the market, which can result in turf injury. Although a good mower will make the task of mowing much easier it is the way that you mow that will create your success or failure. Get rid of the "weekend warrior" mode and think of the mowing as an opportunity to improve the condition of your lawn. Both the frequency of mowing and the height of the mowing are important to how the mowing will affect your turf.

The process of mowing is something that will encourage your grass to be healthier and it actually helps grass to spread out on its own. When you mow grass you cut off the grass tips of the plant. The tips are considered to the apical growing point of the plant. When you mow the tips of the grass plants the response of the turf is to promote lateral growth. The lateral growth will be in the form of rhizomes, stolons, or tillers depending on the type and species of the grass plant. This positive growth occurs if the mowing is done correctly and the grass is not cut too short. If grass plants are mowed closely or "scalped," then negative effects can happen to the grass plants. Mowing will be one of most repeated tasks you will do to your lawn in a growing season, and it must be done correctly each and every time. These are some of the things that can occur when grass is cut too short:

> **PRO POINTER**
> Both the frequency of mowing and the height of the mowing are important to how the mowing will affect your turf.

- Grass is put under stress from moisture loss
- Crowns of the plants can be damaged from sun damage
- Crowns of the grass plants can actually be damaged by the mower
- Weeds are exposed to sunlight where they can easily germinate
- Positive growth can be stifled by the recovery time from scalping
- Turf can become discolored or yellow
- Grass plants can even die

MOWING HEIGHT

The ideal height of the mowing varies by grass type and species. Overall for cool season grasses turf needs to be mowed reasonably tall. Most mowing should be done at a minimum of 2½" in height

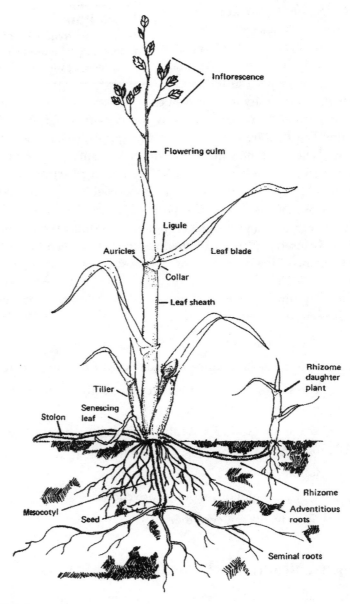

FIGURE 9-1
Being able to identify parts of the grass plant can help you understand what parts can be damaged from mowing.

for optimum conditions in cool season turf. Examples of grass you would cut at this height would include Bluegrass, Ryegrass, and Fescue. When you mow at taller heights you can create several positive effects on the grass. When grass is mowed higher it creates a shading effect which helps to keep weeds from germinating and also protects plant crowns. You can reduce the number of weeds a lawn by 50%–80% by simply raising the mowing height from 2½" to 3½".

Recommended range of mowing heights for the various turf species found in the U.S.

- Bahia grass   2 to 3 inches
- Bentgrass   ⅜ to ¾ inches
- Bermuda grass   ½ to 1½ inches
- Bluegrass   1 ½ to 3½ inches
- Carpet grass   1 to 2 inches
- Centipede grass   1 to 1½ inches
- Fine Fescues   1 to 2½ inches
- Ryegrass   1 to 2½ inches
- St. Augustine grass   1 to 3 inches
- Tall Fescue   2½ to 3½ inches
- Zoysia grass   ½ to 2 inches

These heights are not absolutes but are the heights that will put the least amount of stress on your turf and provide the healthiest looking grass overall. Remember that the shorter ends of the mowing heights will create more weeds and stress to the turfgrass.

> **PRO POINTER**
> You can reduce the number of weeds in a lawn by 50%-80% by simply raising the mowing height from 2 ½" to 3 ½".

Mowing frequency can also affect turf health and reduce the stress of mowing. By mowing more frequently you reduce stress by cutting less of the plant off at a given time. This helps to reduce moisture loss and minimize the shock of cutting the plant in half. If you are cutting a ⅓ or less of the plant off each time it can be very beneficial. It would be much better if you can mow once every four days and cut a little bit of the grass off vs. mowing in eight to ten days and shocking the turf by cutting tall grass very short.

Another positive effect of mowing often is that you will reduce the number of clippings and the size of the clippings. By doing this there will be less chance of thatch build up and a much more attractive appearance to the lawn overall. Thatch is the layer of grass debris that forms on the soil surface that can keep water, fertilizer, and nutrients from entering into the ground. Thatch can create a lot of negative effects in turf quality by literally smothering out the grass after a period of time. A small amount of thatch will always exist on the soil surface which helps to protect plant crowns but if that layer gets too thick it will create problems.

TECH TIP
Thatch is the layer of grass debris that forms on the soil surface that can keep water, fertilizer, and nutrients from entering into the ground.

WHAT TO DO WITH THE GRASS

There are three options for how you can mow your grass and the benefits of each have been debated for years. Different mowing practices fit different circumstances and you should do what works best for you.

The following are your three options for mowing:

- Discharge mowing—Allows grass to be ejected out of the side or rear of the mower in a traditional manner.

- Mulching—This process uses a mower that closes off the deck trapping the grass under the deck to be chopped repeatedly where it is recycled into the soil.

- Bagging—Bagging the grass uses some type of collection system that collects the clippings off of the lawn.

The idea of a side or rear discharge mower encompasses many thoughts regarding the traditional lawn mower. Maybe it is the thought of helping grandpa push a mower around the yard or seeing mom riding the mower around the yard but when people think about a mower this style is the first to come to mind. There is nothing wrong with using this type of mower and each mowing style has its pros and cons. The biggest draw back to using a discharge style of mower is probably an aesthetic one. Typically these types of mowers tend to windrow grass which sits up on top of the lawn like hay. This grass can be heavy if the lawn was mowed when it was tall. Heavy grass clipping can choke out parts of the lawn and lead to thatch problems.

The rate of discharge and dispersal of clippings varies between brands of mowers. If you keep up with the mowing, any side or rear discharge mower can provide an excellent cut and they have been proven to be a reliable type of mower. A rear discharge mower tends to windrow less than a side discharge mower but each will vary based on size and brand. There is a high risk of thrown objects with any mower that ejects grass out of the cutting deck. This is especially true of mowers with a side chute. Use caution and always follow the manufacturer's operator's manual when it comes to operation.

> **TECH TIP**
> The biggest draw back to using a discharge style of mower is probably an aesthetic one.

Mulching grass is a method of mowing that tends to fade in and out of popularity on a regular basis. The concept of mulching is wonderful and it does provide some great benefits to the lawn based on those concepts. The idea of a mulching mower is to trap clippings inside of the mowing deck and continue to chop them into very small pieces which are then recycled into the lawn. By using mulching, valuable water and nutrients are recycled back into the lawn where they can be used by the grass that is still growing. The biggest drawback to the mulching style of mower is that many most homeowners do not mow often enough to maximize the efficiency of a mulching deck.

Mulching requires that you mow every four to five days when grass is actively growing for best results. Since most homeowners only have time to mow once a week or less, by the time many people get

FIGURE 9-2
This style of mower has been around for years and is commonly used as a residential lawn mower.

FIGURE 9-3
This mower is a riding lawn mower that shoots the grass out of the side chute.

the time to mow, the clippings are more than the mower can actually handle. If you allow the grass to get ahead of you one time you may find a certain degree of hay on the lawn for weeks to come. The grass may swirl around under the deck and even come out from under the mower in huge globs when you cut tall grass. If you find that you are the type of person that can stick to a routine mowing regiment a mulching system might work well for you. If you find yourself to be a procrastinator who will not mow regular enough I would suggest an alternative style of mower unless you like fighting clumps of grass. Some mowers that have less horse power might even bog down if the grass gets tall enough. You do limit the risk of thrown object with mulching decks because there is less risk of blades throwing an object such as a rock.

A bagging mower gives you the best aesthetic appearance by far of any of the mowers that you can use. The process of bagging grass keeps debris off the lawn and picks up other debris that can accumu-

FIGURE 9-4
A mulching mower recycles clippings and reduces the risk of thrown objects.

late in the lawn. A huge benefit of bagging mowers is that they pick up and collect weed seeds that other mowers redistribute into the lawn to grow. By collecting the grass the number of weeds can be drastically reduced in the lawn. There are also other benefits of collecting clippings. When clippings are collected thatch build up tends to be minimized in the lawn, however, thatch can still build up in bagged lawns so do not assume that bagging eliminates thatch completely.

The biggest drawback to a bagging mower is that when you collect the clippings you are also collecting the nutrients and water that are found in grass clippings. The clippings off of a lawn are high in Nitrogen and since grass is composed mostly of water you are removing valuable moisture off of the lawn each time you collect the clippings. This may create more of a need for supplemental irrigation and fertilizer over time. If you are already applying fertilizers to your lawn in an application program and you have the ability to water your lawn it is doubtful you would ever see any negative effects from collecting grass clippings.

TYPES OF MOWERS

There are a wide variety of brands of mowers and many different styles in each brand. You should be aware of the three main ways a lawn mower can cut.

These are the three cutting types of lawn mowers

- Reel mower
- Flail mower
- Rotary mower

A reel mower uses a scissors-like action that pinches the grass between a rotating blade and a sharpened cutting edge known as a bed knife. The reel mower is the first type of lawn mower that was ever used and the concept behind the mower does not even require the unit to have a motor to operate the machine. Reel mowers today are still very common for golf course use and athletic fields but it is very unlikely you will find reel mowers used for mowing the lawn.

Figure 9-5
This type of mower picks up clippings which is very aesthetically pleasing.

Reel mowers do provide the best cut quality that is available which is why they are used in professional atmospheres where the best cut quality is required. The problem with these types of mowers is that they are fairly high in maintenance and they require frequent adjustments to keep the cut quality you desire.

A flail mower is a type of mower that has some of the features of a reel mower with a spinning cutting device but unlike the reel mower the flail mower has blades that hang down and cut the grass off as it is rotating. These mowers are used by highway departments because they are very unlikely to throw debris. Unlike a rotary mower, a flail mower is spinning toward the ground, which means that should something be picked up by one of these mowers it is just thrown toward that ground. This mower would almost never be used for lawns but you should be aware that this type of cutting system exists.

The most common type of cutting system used is the rotary mower. Rotary mowers can come in styles that allow bagging, mulching, or that discharge the grass. A rotary mower is the most common style of mower used and almost all lawns are cut with some type of a rotary mower. Rotary mowers do not give you the best cut quality possible, although this is really not a known fact. Rotary mowers have a sharpened blade that spins very fast in a circle. These blades actually tear off the grass although it is considered to be cutting the grass. This is not nearly as clean of a cut as what a reel mower provides. The top edges of the grass blades are cut much smoother with a reel mower than with a rotary mower.

FIGURE 9-6
Reel mowers that are used today range from small 18" mowers up to mowers that are several feet wide which are used on golf courses.

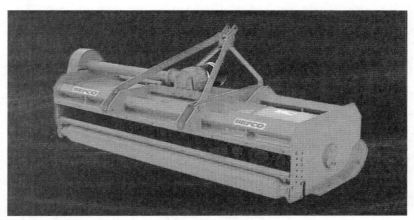

FIGURE 9-7
This type of mower spins and cuts off the grass as it rotates.

Whatever types of mowing you are using for your lawn, remembe, that it is an important part of the maintenance of the lawn. Maintenance of your yard should include the following practices:

- Routine mowing at the correct height and frequency

- Proper fertilization at times throughout the calendar year

- A strict chemical application schedule for weed control

- Routine watering or irrigating when it is needed only

- Overseeding the lawn once a year if possible to introduce new varieties of grass and reduce the number of bare spots that develop in the lawn

- Using some type of power rake or aerator to eliminate thatch and improve turf quality in the fall of each year

- Edging walks and other trimming for aesthetic reasons

- Maintaining the proper soil ph and fertility by doing a soil test and adding lime every three years if needed.

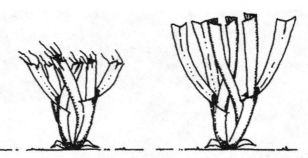

FIGURE 9-8
The figure on the left shows what the grass tip might look like that has been cut with a rotary mower. The figure on the right would be typical of a grass tip that has been cut with a reel mower.

10

Aeration and Dethatching

There are many things that are done to the lawn that are done out of necessity. There are other things that can be done to the lawn that are not really necessary but they can make your lawn be the most outstanding lawn in the neighborhood. It is the few things that you are doing different than others that will make your lawn the showcase of the neighborhood that everyone else wants. You should really focus on a couple of things that should be implemented into your maintenance program on a yearly basis. These things are aeration and dethatching.

Most people understand what the process of aeration is but there are several types of aeration that you can do and each process is different. The overall results from any form of aeration are essentially the same but the methods you can use to achieve aeration are quite different.

These are some methods of aeration you can use

- Core aeration—This method uses a machine that pulls plugs of soil out of the ground

- Deep tine aeration—This process uses a hollow tine which pulls plugs or a solid tine system but the purpose to provide very deep channels into the soil which can improve the entire soil profile

- Spiker aeration—This is the process where you pull a device that uses spiked wheels on a roller which can slice through the soil surface

- Slicer aeration—There are powered machines that use slicing blades to penetrate the soil surface. These machines work good for creating seed beds at the same time

- Solid time aeration—Solid tine aerators poke holes in the soil instead of pulling out plugs of soil. The machines are almost always pulled behind a tractor or mower.

- Hydroject aeration—Although this is more common to golf courses this process uses high pressure water streams to force holes into the soil surface.

Aeration should be done at least once in the fall of each year. Aeration will help to reduce the compaction in soils and keep the turfgrass looking vigorous. Aeration provides many benefits to the lawns condition. The reduction of soil compaction is one of the biggest benefits that aeration can provide. Traffic on a lawn from mowers, feet, and other heavy equipment over time can compact soils. Soil compaction will naturally increase over a period of time unless something is done to relieve the soil compaction. The more traffic an area gets the worse that compaction will be. For instance, construction or unusual traffic will multiply the effects of the compaction to an area. Earth worm activity is one of the few things that provide natural aeration in nature. If you have a healthy population of worms, your soil may not be as compacted as other soils, but any lawn can benefit from aeration so you should consider making it part of your annual routine for lawn maintenance.

Another huge benefit from aeration is that it will help to eliminate thatch problems. Aeration reduces thatch by redistributing soil over the top of the grass which is a great way to increase the microbial activity that gets rid of thatch in the turf. Core aeration is good

FIGURE 10-1
This type of aerator can cover a large area and it is fairly inexpensive to own.

because there is also the added benefit of leveling that occurs from the redistribution of the soil plugs. As the plugs are broken down on the soil surface the low spots get filled in and the overall effect is a gradual leveling process. Keep in mind that this is gradual and you should not expect aeration to solve unlevel areas overnight. There are huge benefits to using some form of aeration in a turfgrass maintenance schedule. The overall turf quality will be incomparable on a lawn that has been aerated compared to one that has not. Aeration can also be used in combination with a seeding procedure to eliminate bare spots and to improve the thickness of your lawn.

DID YOU KNOW?
Core aeration is good because there is also the added benefit of leveling that occurs from the redistribution of the soil plugs.

Overseeding should also be performed at least once in the fall of each year in combination of aeration or by using a slicing seeder. This is especially helpful with cool season lawns that contain Fescue, Bluegrass, or Ryegrass. Overseeding should be done to rid the lawn of bare spots and to introduce newer varieties of turf into the yard each year. Newer varieties of grass tend to have better qualities such as greener color, better disease resistance, and insect resistance.

Aeration is very helpful to the lawn and provides several benefits

- Reduces compacted soils
- Allows water to permeate the soil
- Allows nutrients from fertilizers to move into the soil
- Increases soil porosity and air flow with the turf roots
- Creates a leveling of the soil over time by allowing soil to be redistributed into low spots
- Provides a seed bed for new grass seed by improving seed to soil contact.

There are solid tine aerators and hollow core aerators which both provide aeration to the soil. Any aerator that pulls a plug out of the soil gives you more benefit than a device that slices the soil or punches a hole in the soil. You can expect to get much more relief of a compaction problem, thatch removal, and other things by actually pulling cores out of the ground. Any form of aeration will be greatly beneficial to your lawn so utilize any aeration device that you have access to.

There is very new type of aeration that is being used more and more each year and although it is more common in sports turf, and golf courses, it is used in lawn care. This aeration process is known as hydroject aeration. This procedure uses high pressure water streams to penetrate the soil to alleviate compaction problems. Be aware of such methods as technology creates new procedures to provide aeration in lawns.

Another method that is more common to golf course use than lawns is deep tine aeration. This type of aeration is usually done in

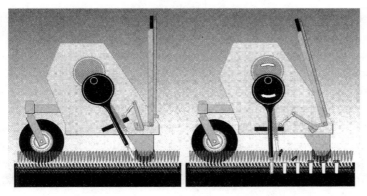

Transport/Retracted   *Operating*

FIGURE 10-2
There are many benefits from the core pulling process of aeration.

FIGURE 10-3
Hydroject aerators use high pressure water streams to fracture
the soil surface and relieve soil compaction.

the spring because recovery from deep tine aeration is much faster at this time of the year. Deep tine aerators can pull plugs or use a solid tine. Solid deep tine aeration is less disruptive to the lawn because it does not create as much of a mess as a core pulling process. If you have a severe compaction issue with your lawn, deep tine aeration is way to change your whole soil profile without having to till up the lawn and start from scratch. Either type of deep tine aeration creates deep channels which can reach up to 18" deep in the soil. Core pulling creates a faster more drastic effect. By filling these holes with sand, channels are created for fast drainage of surface water. When you fill the holes with sand the process is known as topdressing. If you are dealing with heavily compacted soils the process of filling the holes should be immediate. That will allow the sand channels to reach deeper into the soil. Since many diseases thrive in moist conditions, and pathogens like to reproduce in water, the process of deep tine aeration can make disease occurrence less likely. Deep tine aeration can also move away surface water that may have killed out areas of grass from sitting on the soil surface and drowning the healthy turf. The only draw backs with deep tine aeration is the cost of the process and the risk of hitting something in the soil because of the depth of the penetration of the tines.

The core aeration process is something that can be very beneficial to older lawns and it is also great for reducing thatch in all lawns. It will relieve compacted soils and help to improve damaged areas that may develop from year to year. When doing core aeration typically an aerator is used that pulls plugs and deposits them on the soil surface. Aerators for lawns use a rolling action that pulls the plugs out of the ground. As the machine rolls, the weight of the machine pushes out the plugs as it goes along. Some lawn aerators use a piston type action that pulls the plugs out of the ground. There can be a problem with dealing with the core debris that is pulled from the lawns with many piston-type aerators because so many more cores are pulled. If a deep tine aerator is used to pull plugs, debris plugs are left on top of the soil and can even be more extensive, which can require the assistance of a slicing device to break up the cores.

FIGURE 10-4
Example of a deep tine aerator.

Dealing with cores can easily be done with a power raking device or some other sort of machine that has vertical slicing. Golf courses use mowers called verticutters which have reels that slice up the cores and the surface of the grass. Some of these slicing devices can be used for the aeration process itself. A power raking type device is great for relieving light compaction issues and creating a wonderful seed bed before spreading new grass seed. These machines work well for dealing with core problems that other types of core aerators leave behind. By shredding up the core material, the leveling effect on the lawn is a little more immediate. You should not look to the aeration process as a short term way to level up an uneven lawn.

A power rake is a very versatile device when it comes to lawn care. These are some of the things a power rake can do.

- Dethatching
- Loosen light compaction
- Shred aeration cores
- Prepare the lawn for overseeding by creating a seed bed

Power raking is a great way to dethatch a lawn if you have access to one. You might be a little overwhelmed with the debris you will turn up out of a yard if you have never used a power rake before. A power rake has a thrashing action that scratches the soil surface while removing the layer of thatch at the same time. This thatch can accumulate on the soil for years, so in some cases you can turn up a tremendous amount of thatch debri,s which you will have to rake up or bag up with some type of collection device.

There are many other dethatching devices available to remove debris in the lawn. Some devices are called lawn combers and others are just referred to as lawn dethatchers. All of the devices use some mechanical action to thrash the soil surface bringing the compacted thatch material up to the top. As long as you are doing this type of procedure you are benefiting the lawn a great deal. The removal of thatch is your goal; no matter what device you are trying to use.

Keep in mind that once thatch is removed you will see several benefits from removing it. Thatch can really put up a road block to the progress of getting your lawn in shape. This is especially true when trying to revitalize older lawns that may just need a "face lift." Keep in mind that a routine aeration should be scheduled at least once a year.

Many people do not have access to an aerator, power rake, or a dethatching device. This may be why so many people to use this type

of device in their lawn maintenance schedule. You can easily rent
a device like this by the day, or
even by the week, if you need one
for a longer period of time. You
should really seek a way to find
access to this type of machine if
you are not using anything to relieve
soil compaction and thatch problems in your lawn.

DID YOU KNOW?
Processes that disturb the soil surface make barrier forming herbicides useless.

Keep in mind that there is a certain time of the year you should
do aeration or dethatching to the lawn. This would be either very
early in the spring or any time in the fall. The fall is still the best time
for most types of aeration because you can incorporate some type of
seeding process along with your aeration or dethatching process. If
you have no choice other than doing your aeration in the spring then
try to do it very early. Processes that disturb the soil surface make barrier forming herbicides useless. If you are trying to implement a weed
control program, crabgrass controls need to be put down very early
in the year. In most cases this would be prior to the first part of April
in most regions. It is tough to juggle seeding, aeration, and weed control in the short window you have available in the early spring of the
year. These processes will work against each other if you try to do
them too close together. Herbicides will prohibit seed germination if
you do not allow four weeks of time between seeding time, and application time.

It may take a little more time to use an aerator or dethatching
device, but the results you will see in your lawn will be well worth the
extra work. These processes work to improve the soil and the turf
condition at the same time. There is a type of aeration that may be
more suited for your needs and for your lawn's needs, as well as the
availability of various equipment in your geographic area.

11

Weeds in the Lawn

By far the most important part of lawn care is taking care of weeds in the lawn. Weed control is something that you need to keep up from month-to-month and year-to-year. That means that you cannot take time off from your weed control program and expect the lawn to remain in good condition. Weeds are persistent problems when it comes to lawn care, and it takes a very short period of time for weeds to take over the entire yard. Many weeds germinate in a matter of hours when exposed to moisture and some weed seeds have been proven to be viable for as many as 18 years or more.

Many weeds reproduce at rates that allow them to dominate an area in a matter of weeks. Weeds require little moisture to germinate and they are much more resourceful than turfgrass is in competing for survival. Weeds can germinate in hot or dry

> **PRO POINTER**
> Many weeds germinate in a matter of hours when exposed to moisture, and some weed seeds have been proven to be viable for as many as 18 years or more.

weather, and most have extensive roots to insure their survival in almost all environmental conditions. A crabgrass plant can produce up to 10,000 seeds in a growing season, so if only a few plants live through a growing season then the problems can multiply without a proper weed control program. Even the most beautiful lawns can fall victim to weed problems for a variety of reasons. The best looking lawn in the neighborhood can quickly become the local eye sore from a change of residence, from a lawn fanatic to someone who is not concerned with weed control at all.

WEED CONTROL

Most people would like to see a situation where there are no weeds in the lawn at all, but this type of mentality can lead to excessive pesti-

FIGURE 11-1
While this crabgrass plant may seem insignificant, it is capable of producing thousands of viable seeds in just one season.

cide usage in some cases. Weed control success is relevant to what is going on in the areas around the location you are trying to control the weeds in. For instance, the best weed control program in the world may not be that successful if none

DID YOU KNOW?
A weed in the lawn can be defined simply as a plant out of place.

of the adjoining properties are controlling weeds at all. Weed control needs to be done with a program that uses fertilizers to encourage vigorous turf growth. In combination with pre-emergents and contact herbicides, you can target weeds throughout a yearly program. Weed control is relevant to the type of turf area that is being controlled. 100 percent weed control would be the expectation for a golf course green but would be an unlikely goal for a 10-acre property. This is not to say that 100 percent control is not always the desired effect, however, the cost to have such weed control is often impractical and unlikely in most cases. Also, never forget that the over usage of pesticides has environmental implications.

RECOGNIZING WEEDS

A weed in the lawn can be defined simply as a plant out of place. This is relevant to where the plant is growing and if it matches its surroundings. A fescue plant would not be considered a weed if it was in with thousands of other fescue plants in a lawn, but if that same fescue plant was in a ryegrass lawn it would appear horribly out of place. Most people recognize what they consider to be common weeds in their lawn, but everyone's view of what a weed might be is different. For the most part, when people think of weeds they think more along the lines of controlling Crabgrass, Dandelions, or even ground ivy in the lawn. A golf course superintendent might have thoughts of weed control of a plant known as Poa annua or Annual Ryegrass. No matter what the definition of a weed is to you, the most important thing is how to control the weed and when to control them.

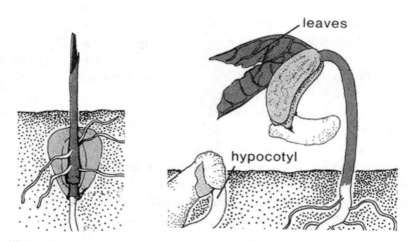

FIGURE 11-2
Diagram of an emerging grass plant on left and a dicot weed with labels.

Weeds can be classified into categories for all practical identification purposes:

- Annual grasses (monocot weeds)—Moncot weeds come from a single plant cotyledon. The monocots include many undesirable grasses that can occur in turfgrass. Examples of some grassy weeds would be Crabgrass, Goosegrass, and Bermuda grass.

- Broadleaf weeds (dicot weeds)—There are dicot weeds which are weeds that come from a plant with two cotyledons. Examples of this type of weed include Dandelion, Plantain, Purple Violet, and Clover.

- Sedges—These are not true grass plants although their appearance may resemble a grass. These plants come from underground bulbs. Examples of sedges are yellow and purple Nutsedge.

Weeds also can be classified based on the blooming habits of the weeds. There are three classifications for weeds based on how they bloom:

- Annuals—Annuals take only one growing season to come into bloom and they only live for a growing season. This time-frame can be defined by the time between the last spring frost and first fall frost in the Northern regions.

- Biennials—These weeds take one year to grow and establish and then bloom during the second growing season. They will complete their growing cycle within two growing seasons.

- Perennials—This weed type will persist from year to year and it can bloom the first year and every year after that.

Annual grass weeds are controlled in different ways than what dicot broadleaf weeds are controlled. Grassy weeds are controlled with a pre-emergent herbicide in most instances which puts down a barrier to prevent the weed seeds from germinating. The barrier that is created keeps the weed seeds from germinating as long as this barrier is not disrupted. If this soil barrier is ever disturbed then new weed seeds could possibly germinate. An herbicide barrier can be broken by things such as:

- Weed eater contact on soil along sidewalk edges
- Cleats on shoes, especially in athletic fields
- Excessive amounts of rain
- Mower or vehicle tire tracking
- Any form of cultivation or tilling

There are other herbicides that provide post-emergence control of grassy weeds, but there are not nearly as many choices available as pre-emergent herbicides, and they often only work on grassy weeds in the younger stages of growth before the grass plants tiller or get very large. This means that a late application of a product to control a grassy weed problem is not going to be nearly as successful as an early application. An example of a pre-emergent chemical would be Pendemethalin, which is a very old chemical name that has been successful for controlling crabgrass for many years. An example of a post emergent control for crabgrass and other annual grasses would be known as Dythiopyr. Dythiopyr is sold under the trade name Dimension and it will provide post emergence control of crabgrass as long as it is not in the mature tillering stage. Dythiopyr also provides pre-emergent control of crabgrass but its most desirable feature is the fact that is one of the few chemicals that provide post emergence control after seeds have germinated. There are new products available that are providing control later in the growing season, but as temperatures increase the stress increases on desirable turf.

One very good thing about the control of annual grasses is that you basically get to start with a clean slate from year to year. There are always viable seeds waiting to germinate from year to year but a killing frost will take care of these weed types from one calendar year to the next. Perennial weeds will stay green in the winter and live from year to year where annual grasses cannot survive freezing temperatures. This means that you can implement a better weed control strategy the next year if you do not have success with what you are currently trying to accomplish.

Many turfgrass professionals who treat lawns for annual grasses use a double or split application of pre-emergent chemical or an application of pre-emergent chemical early in the spring followed by a post emergent treatment later in the spring. Either method will work for controlling annual grasses in turfgrass. It is not possible to wait until late in the season to think about crabgrass control. Without some sort of early chemical treatment in the Midwest, Crabgrass is almost a guaranteed problem. Since one Crabgrass plant can produce thousands of seeds per season, even a handful of plants can produce one million viable seeds for the following season. Crabgrass is the number one weed in the United States so you should be aware of how to control it. Crabgrass is often referred to by the incorrect name of Water Grass.

Dicot weeds in the lawn are referred to as broadleaf weeds and the methods of control are quite different than with grassy weeds. Broadleaf weeds need to be controlled after they germinate instead of

FIGURE 11-3
Crabgrass is the number one weed problem in the U.S. Ironically it is not even native to the United States.

before they germinate. Broadleaves are much easier to control in the seedling stage so early control of broadleaf weeds does have its benefits. By controlling broadleaves early in the year you prevent the plants from seeding out and creating more viable seeds that can germinate in the lawn. Broadleaves can become more resistant to chemical control as they mature through late spring and into the summer months; however the fall is also a good time to control broadleaf weeds. The reason fall is a good time is because weeds are in the process of gathering energy and creating food for survival during the long winter months. At this time they are very vulnerable to chemical control.

The most commonly known control for broadleaf weeds would be the chemical known as 2, 4-D which has been around for years. Typically this chemical is used in combination with MCPP and Dicamba in a mixture which can be sold under a variety of trade names. One popular combination of these three chemicals is available in a product which is known as Trimec™. By combining chemicals together a wider range of weeds can be controlled. Any of these products individually will provide you with reasonable control of broadleaf weeds, but combined, the success of control is much better.

FIGURE 11-4
Although this bottle reads "Weed Out," the active ingredient in
the bottle is Trimec.

Sedges are not controlled by the same chemicals that are used to control grasses or broadleaf weeds. There are only a few chemicals that can be used for sedge control in lawns. One example of a successful control currently used or Nutsedge control is a chemical known as Manage . There are new technologies that will hopefully create new chemicals that will control all major weeds in one bottle but currently the choices are limited. Sedges are quite resilient because they are able to spread by rhizomes, seed, and under the ground by spreading bulblets. Treatment for sedges can be very costly so you may want to choose to spot treat your problems areas instead of treating the entire lawn.

FIGURE 11-5
Many people who have good weed control programs cannot get rid of Nutsedge because the chemicals they use do not work on this weed.

PESTICIDE TREATMENT SCHEDULES

Following is an application schedule for cool season turfgrass:

- Late February–Mid March: Pre-emergent treatment on fertilizer for annual grasses which would include Crabgrass
- Mid March–Mid May: Post emergent broadleaf application. You can apply one application early in April and a second one in late May if your broadleaf problem is bad.
- Early May–Late May: Post emergent treatment on fertilizer for annual grasses and Crabgrass
- Mid May–Early August: Grub control (sometimes with fertilizer if performed before June 1st)
- September–Early October: Optional Post emergent broadleaf application if no seeding work is planned. This is an alternative to doing two applications for broadleaves in the spring and only should be used if no fall seeding is planned.
- Late August–Late November: Fall fertilizing can be in two applications. Lime applications should be applied in the fall if a soil test indicates the need for a ph adjustment.

Typical schedule for warm season turf in lawn care follows:

- Mid March–Mid May: Post emergent broadleaf application. Usually one application is sufficient in warm season grass but two applications can be used with a bad problem with weeds.
- Early May–Late May: Post emergent treatment on fertilizer for annual grasses which includes Crabgrass
- Mid May–Early August: Grub control (sometimes with fertilizer depending on your warm season program). Mid-summer fertilizing is acceptable in warm season turf.
- August: Last fertilizing of season - no more than one pound of N per 1,000
- September–October: Second broadleaf application if it was not performed in the spring. Possible lime application if a ph test would indicate the need for one

You should make a decision if you believe you can handle the application of pesticides on your own. Handling herbicides for weed control takes a lot of care and caution when you apply them. One misapplication can harm non target pests or cause damage to plants, animals, and people. Broadleaf herbicides tend to be very volatile which means they can move off site and damage plants that were not intended to be sprayed. One way to help minimize this type of drift is by purchasing an Amine or salt formulation of broadleaf herbicide instead of an ester formulation. Ester formulations of the chemical 2, 4-D are highly volatile and most were intended for agricultural use instead of lawn care use.

A skilled professional might be a better alternative to taking care of your weed control needs. Sometimes a professional can apply your treatments for close to the cost of what you would spend to buy the product yourself. It is important to weigh the risks of handling chemicals yourself vs. hiring someone else to do the job. Pesticide application cost varies drastically from city to city, so cost could be a deciding factor in your decision. Always remember that if you choose to handle chemicals yourself you should always read the label and follow safe handling instructions for using the herbicide.

> **PRO POINTER**
> Ester formulations of the chemical 2, 4-D are highly volatile and most were intended for agricultural use instead of lawn care use.

ALTERNATIVES TO WEED CONTROL PESTICIDES

Alternatives to pesticide usage are becoming very popular because of concepts such as integrated pest management and other practices that encourage less frequent use of chemicals. IPM, as it is known, would suggest a person treat for weeds on a have to basis and to try to use preventative practices and chemical alternatives. In other words chemicals are only used once thresholds are reached.

The threshold is measured based on:

- Damage factor

- Financial factors

- Esthetic factor

The deciding commonality between these three issues is when the damage from any pest or disease reaches an intolerable point. Organic based herbicides are available and new technologies are creating safer chemicals each year. Since organics rely on the natural things that are found in our environment they are more desirable for use by people with a low appreciation for chemical use. It is possible to use things to reduce weeds in the lawn like collection of grass clippings and mowing the lawn at a much higher height. By using cultural practices you could at least reduce the amount of chemicals applied to the lawn and still achieve a desirable result.

Pest Management for Turfgrass

Pest management in turf can be viewed in many different ways. There are some people that would view one of any pest in the lawn to be one too many. A pest can have many definitions when it comes to turfgrass management and care. Pests can be weeds, insects, diseases, animals, or anything that is considered to interfere with the appearance or something that causes economic injury to the lawn and landscape. All pests are controlled based on what ever level you choose to be the threshold for control. This method takes IPM or Integrated Pest Management decisions into consideration instead of just treating for 100% control of all pests that are encountered. It would be considered to be more acceptable to use thresholds for controlling pests instead of an eradication method for removing all pests. Eradication is the concept of trying to eliminate all of a certain type of pest.

EVASIVE SPECIES

Pests can fall into different levels of being controlled. A hand full of certain pests can be tolerated if they are not causing severe damage or if they are not considered to be a pest that can spread out of control. Evasive species considered to be pests that are persistent problem pests that sometimes reproduce at a high rate. These pests often are not controlled by normal control strategies. In many cases the pest may spread uncontrollably without some form of control. Following are some examples of an evasive pest species:

- New insect is discovered that is not controllable with traditional chemicals that are on the market.

- A weed that is present in the landscape or lawn that has a tremendous ability to spread on its own. It may possess many ways to reproduce such as stolons, rhizomes, and seed.

- An insect develops resistance to traditional insecticides and does a huge amount of damage while a new control measure is discovered.

- New plant is introduced to an area that is not native to an area and reproduces at a rapid rate.

- A disease occurs that at first is not even diagnosable. This progresses into a serious problem before a new fungicide is developed.

There are numerous examples of how any pest can become an evasive species. Evasive species are not limited to any one type of pest that exists and can include all categories of pests. The issue of evasive species introduced intentionally or accidentally can always create a potential problem to an eco-system or an environment. Imported species have been an especially challenging problem for decades if not centuries.

TECH TIP
The issue of evasive species introduced intentionally or accidentally can always create a potential problem to an eco-system or an environment.

CONSEQUENCES OF INFESTATION

The situation of non-native species having their way with new environments has been the subject of some nightmarish stories and tragic consequences that are historically notorious in creating ecological havoc to this day. The list of problem species that have found their way to non-native shores, and the destructive path they have followed, make for some tragic outcomes in the forests, meadows, waterways, agronomic fields and landscapes that are well documented and still unfolding at present.

The newspapers, televisions and radio accounts of these interlopers make for stories that read right out of science fiction scenarios, but they are unfortunately all too real. Perhaps the worst, and most potentially catastrophic, development when an introduced species meets with a new ecosystem is the potential for virtual extinction and/or displacement of native population with little chance of recovery once the damage has been done.

For as long as there has been commerce, trade and cultural exchanges between cultures there has been both the potential, as well as realized, situation of inadvertent, if not intentional, introduction of species into ranges for which nature had not intended. This occurs when new plants are discovered in areas outside of the site to which they are native. People then feel a desire to introduce these plants into a home or lawn that may be located hundreds of miles away if not thousands of miles from their native site. This is one reason that commerce in to and out of the United States is monitored so closely. There needs to be a constant monitoring for potential evasive species whether it is the check points at our borders or the inspections of the freighters that hit our ocean ports.

The list is long when it comes to plants, animals and diseases that have gained footholds in ecological communities for which no natural enemies or biotic controls can limit populations or adaptations to new environments. The very selectivity and delicate balance that characterizes a particular bio-system makes the vulnerability to new species especially sensitive. The lack of outside control in the form of

FIGURE 12-1
Insects can stow away overseas in crating materials.

disease, virus, predators and abiotic factors plays a crucial role in whether or not an organism will find a new home in strange surroundings. The situations are elevated to seriousness if there are no unnatural or natural controls for the spread of any species. The mere existence of one natural enemy may be the one limiting factor deciding whether or not an organism thrives, merely exists or barely hangs on. If man has no ability to limit the spread of a species the consequences can be magnified ten fold.

DISEASE PROBLEMS IN A LAWN

Disease control is usually more applicable to golf courses or turfgrass in an athletic field. It is often impractical to treat for diseases in lawn care unless there is an unusual situation where severe economic injury to the lawn is possible. Economic thresholds are a common measure of when chemical treatments may outweigh the alterna-

PRO POINTER
Economic thresholds are a common measure of when chemical treatments may outweigh the alternative.

tive. There are numerous diseases which can occur in turfgrass but most of these diseases are only treated on golf courses, athletic fields, or sports complexes.

Disease only occurs when there is a pathogen that has host in the presence of a suitable environment. All three factors must be present before disease is a possibility. Lawns are susceptible to many different plant pathogens but many diseases are never diagnosed or treated in lawn care. There are pathogens that can attack your lawn in every season of the year in some way or another.

The best way to control diseases in the lawn is to focus on cultural practices rather than the use of chemical controls. Disease in the lawn

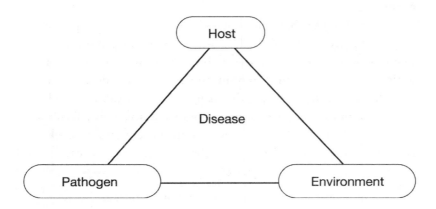

FIGURE 12-2
There must be a host, pathogen, and the correct environment for a disease to actually occur.

is common but the damage is not usually noticed by homeowners unless widespread devastation actually occurs. Lawns are much taller in height than the turf you would typically find on an athletic field or golf course. This creates conditions where the disease may not be as obvious or even noticed.

If you suspect that you have a disease in your lawn one to way to know for sure is through the use of a microscope. Since most people do not own such a device the most logical and feasible way to make this determination is to send the sample to someone who can tell you what your problem is. Most communities have a local extension office that can either help make a diagnosis for you or they can send your sample off to be analyzed at another location. In most cases the sample will eventually end up at a university where it will be looked at by a plant pathologist. It is difficult to diagnose disease with the naked eye but some experienced professionals can help you to determine if you have a problem. Keep in mind that unhealthy grass may not have a disease but it can still appear sick from a range of other problems.

If you discover that you do have a disease, the next step would be to cure the disease problem. The unfortunate thing about disease is that once you have noticed the problem, in most cases some damage is already done. Chemical prevention would be the ideal way to deal with disease but in lawn care that is just not practical. Fungicides are one of the most expensive groups of pesticides that exist. That means that cultural practices are the best way to prevent and control a disease problem. Cultural practices that can prevent disease would include:

- Limit over watering; excess water can encourage disease.
- Always try to water early in the day so grass blades can dry off.
- Make sure the lawn is properly fertilized; too much or too little fertilizer can encourage certain diseases.

- Encourage healthy roots and overall plant health. Healthy plants can fight off disease and have more natural resistance.

- Keep in mind that weakened plants will be more susceptible to disease.

- Make sure air flow is adequate to the lawn areas. Low line areas that remain wet and humid are more likely to develop disease problems

Diseases that are found in the lawn would include:

- Yellow patch (sheath spot, and sheath blight)
- Downy mildew
- Pythium blight
- Red thread
- Brown patch
- Grey leaf spot
- Dollar spot
- Snow mold

Diseases can occur in both warm and cool season turf and they are common in all places in the United States. Keep in mind that many diseases occur in the presence of high temperatures, high humidity, and moist conditions. There are diseases that can occur even when it snows but overall the most destructive disease usually occur in the middle of summer when conditions are at their worst. The best defense against having a disease problem in the lawn is to have a very healthy lawn in the first place.

Something to remember about disease problems in lawns is that the types of diseases and controls change from year to year. Diseases have a great ability to adapt and change which means the control measures for the disease must change also. As new diseases are discovered, the awareness of these problems needs to be widespread so that everyone can recognize, diagnose, and treat for potential epidemics. Always rely on the resources available to you to keep you up to date on current pest and disease problems. Also contact your local extension office to find out if your control strategies and chemicals are the best ones available for your problem. There are several general purpose fungicides that can be purchased under popular name brands. These fungicides might be effective for control but if you do not know exactly what you are trying to treat, then chemicals may be useless.

INSECT CONTROL

Insect control is something that is very important to a golf course superintendent but unfortunately not nearly as big of a priority for homeowners. Insecticide control is not always used in programs for lawn care professionals until damage to the lawn is visible. A yearly insecticide application can be performed to at least control grub worm populations in the lawn.

GRUB WORMS

Grub worms are one of the more common insects to be found in the lawn. Grub damage in the lawn may not be obvious that an insect is the cause of your problem. Often grub damage appears to look like drought damage or maybe just a thinning area at first. There are a variety of grub worms that exist in the lawn and each type of grub takes on a very different form as an adult. For example, most people in the Midwest are very familiar with an insect known as the June bug or June beetle. What they do not realize is that the June beetle is an adult stage of a very common grub worm that can do damage to the lawns. The grubs feed on turfgrass roots and as they mature they get closer and closer to the soil surface. Eventually the grubs molt into June beetles where they can fly around and lay eggs in the soil, starting the whole process over again. The recommended times for treating grub worms have to do with the timeframe when the grubs are highest in the soil profile. Most grubs are highest in the soil profile sometime around the end of May.

Grub worms in a lawn can be controlled with an application of a general purpose insecticide but resistance to older chemicals continues to be an increasing problem. There are also an increasing number of insecticides that are being banned each year which

> **DID YOU KNOW?**
> There are also an increasing number of insecticides that are being banned each year and may make the future control of grubs and insects in general a little more difficult.

may make the future control of grubs and insects in general a little more difficult. Diazinon was one of most recent chemicals to be banned which had been used as an effective grub control on lawns for years. If you are looking for instant grub control the chemical Dylox™ works in a 24-hour period giving you fast and immediate results. Incidentally it also is a great control for many other lawn insects that can be a nuisance in and around the home. If you are

FIGURE 12-3
This is just one the many grub species that can occur in the lawn.

looking for season long control of grubs there are a couple of possible controls. One is a product called Merit™ which will give you season long control (120 days) of grubs when applied at the correct time. If you are looking for a slightly more modern or natural approach there is a product that works in a non-typical mode for successful grub control. That product is known as Mach II ™ which is a hormone that causes the bugs to molt prematurely. When this happens the feeding parts of the grub are covered by premature growth and shedding of the skin so the grubs starve to death. Any of the above products listed will provide exceptional grub control.

CHINCH BUGS

Another insect that might be encountered in the lawn would be chinch bugs. Chinch bugs are not nearly as common in comparison to grubs but when they occur in turfgrass the damage can be devastating. Chinch bugs are a feeding insect that can create very fast damage in the lawn. One mistake I see when it comes to the treatment of chinch bugs is they often winter in off site locations such as home foundations and not in the lawn which makes their control a little more difficult. Some professionals do not take into consideration that the chinch bugs can harbor in and around walk ways and structures therefore treatments of just the turf areas may not be successful. A general purpose insecticide at a high rate will probably rid most turf of chinch bugs but multiple treatments are often necessary. Dylox™ or even a chemical such as Sevin™ will successfully get rid of these bugs.

PRO POINTER
The only good thing about the birds feeding on the bugs is that they can be used as an indicator that an insect problem exists.

CUTWORMS

Cutworms can be a very destructive insect when it comes to the short time frame it takes for them to do significant damage to the turf. Cutworms are also a favorite

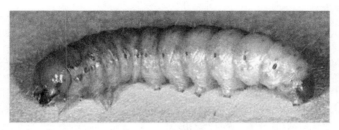

FIGURE 12-4
Cutworms are more of a surface feeding type insect.

food for many bird species, which can also cause turf injury. The
only good thing about the birds feeding on the bugs is that they can
be used as an indicator that an insect problem exists. Cutworms are
root feeding insects that can decimate an area in a very short period
of time. Cutworms are more commonly known for destruction they
cause in agricultural crops but they can cause significant turfgrass
injury as well. A good treatment for the control of cutworms would
be Telstar .

MOLE CRICKET

An interesting insect that can occur in turfgrass is an insect known as
a mole cricket. Mole crickets are usually associated with warmer climates these insects have been found now in Northern Missouri and
in Central Illinois. Mole crickets are burrowing insects that create
tunnels that look like tiny mole runs in shorter grasses. They are especially bad on golf course where the mole cricket tunnels interfere with
the putting surface of the green. Mole crickets are also difficult to
control and require fairly high rates of insecticides to get rid of the
insects. The size of the mole cricket is impressive to see if you ever

FIGURE 12-5
This insect is more common in southern parts of the United States.

come across one of these bugs. Mole crickets can reach sizes of two to three inches in length but commonly they are in the 1½ inches range. Mature adults can develop wings which allow them to be able to easily move to new locations. Mild winters and global warming may be causing movement into Northern regions.

There are other lawn insects that can be found in the lawn but overall the control measures are fairly similar. Be aware that insects are very adaptable creatures that have survived since the beginnings of time. They can adapt, change, and build up resistance to control methods. One way to help prevent resistance is to alternate the type of insecticides you are using each time instead of using the same ones over and over.

OTHER PESTS PROBLEMS IN TURFGRASS

The one thing that most pest problems have in common when it comes to turfgrass is that they can be solved by using some type of chemical treatment. There are however many pests that cannot be controlled with chemicals. There are other pests that can be controlled with chemicals only not very successfully. This is when management strategies become your only defense in getting rid of the pests or perhaps using alternatives to chemicals are needed.

MOLES

Moles are one of the most difficult pests to control where some type of chemical will not fix the problem. Methods for controlling voles, moles, and gophers are all very similar. Each of these pests shares a distinctive feature which makes them very difficult to control. That underlying issue is that all of these animals are mammals which make chemical usage unpredictable, dangerous, and unsuccessful. The distinction with being a mammal is that humans, pets, and livestock are also mammals, which means that non-target injury could be dangerous or potentially deadly to humans. Most of the products that have traditionally been available for controlling moles and other underground dwelling varmints are in the fumigant family. This means that in all actuality, in most states, a special fumigant license is required to use the types of chemicals needed to control these pests even though the pests are considered to be lawn pests.

> **TECH TIP**
> The distinction with being a mammal is that humans, pets, and livestock are also mammals, which means that non-target injury could be dangerous or potentially deadly to humans.

Moles are very difficult to control even with the use of such fumigants. Fumigants are used in a trial and error fashion which may require several attempts to even hit any of the target pests. In the meantime there is repeated risk to the non target animals encountering these materials. The problem and danger with most baits, poisons, and fumigants is that they contain potentially toxic active ingredients which could kill a human if exposure was severe enough. All pesticides have potential risks to humans and off target pests but the products used to control moles could be lethal in very small quantities to any mammal that encounters them. Just one accidental exposure to these products could be fatal and that means that use of these products should be done very cautiously.

FIGURE 12-6
Many homeowners do not know how or what to do about moles so they give up and let the moles take over a property.

Some of the products used contain active ingredients like Strychnine, Arsenic, Aluminum Phosphate or some other hazardous or poisonous substance.

If a fumigant is used it must be used in the areas that are showing the most recent signs of mole activity. Moles are one of the hardest pests to control that you will encounter in a lawn. They are a frustration for home owners as well as the people who try to control them. A fresh mole run is the first place you should start treating for moles, because moles do not always travel through older runs. Poison pellets or fumigant tablets are deposited on the inside of the runs every 5 to 10 feet in hope that the moles will come into contact with the material or the gas that is released by the products. If you are treating older runs or areas where the moles are not active then you will not be successful. This is where the trial and error comes into effect. You must continue to treat the fresh runs until you do not see any further activity or damage to the lawn in that area. While you are treating these runs you run the risk of a pet digging into the run and coming into contact with the material that was intended to kill the moles. It is a rare possibility that a human could also encounter this material but it is highly unlikely.

PRO POINTER
If you are treating older runs or areas where the moles are not active then you will not be successful.

DID YOU KNOW?
If the mole is leaving a long straight run then it may not be finding much for a food source. On the other hand if the mole is making a zigzag pattern in the lawn where it is causing a lot of damage, chances are there is a plentiful source of grubs in that area and the mole may be planning on sticking around for a while.

POCKET GOPHERS

Pocket gophers are another species of destructive animals to get into the lawn. Pocket gophers are the animals that make the huge mounds of dirt in the yard that cause havoc for lawn mowers. These mounds are the result of the gophers cleaning out all of the runs and rooms and excavating the soil out of one opening at the soil level. This large mound causes a lot of difficulties for mowers and creates an unattractive appearance in the lawn. It does make it a little easier to treat for pocket gophers when it comes to finding the more active mounds and runs. One good mowing or leveling off of the ground will quickly reveal which runs are being used on a daily basis. The pocket gophers will visit what are considered to be underground room areas regularly. These rooms are sometimes very low in the soil profile and they can provide an excellent place for the animals to survive during the winter. Gophers are often mistaken for moles by homeowners but in all actuality they are two completely different animals.

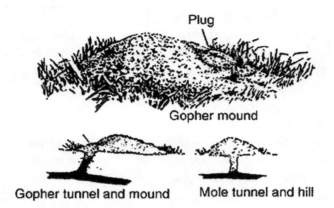

Plug

Gopher mound

Gopher tunnel and mound   Mole tunnel and hill

FIGURE 12-7
Pocket gophers leave very noticeable signs that they have invaded the lawn by cleaning out the runs and leaving large piles of dirt.

Traps

Traps are another option for the control of moles but they have very limited success against pocket gophers. Since moles make long runs in the lawn there is a way to set a trap so the mole will run through the trap. With the case of pocket gophers it is hard to get the animals to encounter the trap just by the way they behave. There is one mistake that people make when setting traps for moles. The best way to set a mole trap is to take your foot and smash down three to four feet of the run to close it off. Then put either a snare- or spike-type trap in the middle of the area you have smashed down. When the mole tries to open the run back up it will encounter the trap and set it off. It is very unlikely that the mole will encounter the trap if the soil is not smashed down first. This is where most homeowners usually makes a mistake in the method of setting the trap. It is very hard to get the mole to encounter the trap without smashing down the soil first.

Most moles and gophers feed on the grub worms in the lawn so there is a way to discourage moles and gophers from entering the lawn. Moles and gophers may move off site by eliminating the major food source in a particular area. A good grub treatment each year is a great way to discourage moles from coming into an area and tearing up the lawn. One way to judge mole activity in the lawn is by monitoring the run activity. Moles will leave two types of run patterns when they enter an area. If the mole is leaving a long straight run then it may not be finding much for a food source. On the other hand, if the mole is making a zigzag pattern in the lawn where it is causing a lot of damage, chances are there is a plentiful source of grubs in that area and the mole may be planning on sticking around for a while. If you have applied a grub treatment to the lawn, moles may enter the lawn briefly and then quickly exist once it is discovered there is not a good food source available. This may be evident by a long straight run entering the yard that quickly turns around and exits the same way.

GROUND SQUIRRELS AND OTHER ABOVE-GROUND ANIMALS

Ground squirrels are animals that could cause damage to the lawn but they are difficult to control by using a fumigant or poison bait. Trapping can be successful and can be done with a cage type trap with bait in the trap which attracts them into the trap where they are captured. This method can also work on ground hogs, skunks, and raccoons. Many above ground animals eat bugs and while they are furrowing around looking for food they can cause a great deal of damage to the turf. Skunks are one the more notorious animals for damaging turf while looking for grub worms; especially on golf courses. This is still another reason to make sure you have eliminated grubs in your turfgrass.

CONCLUSION

There are many pests that can be encountered in the lawn. Some people consider deer to even be a pest in the lawn due to the damage that is caused by their hoofed feet. Whatever the measure of a pest is to you be sure that you are managing your problems in an effective manner that uses chemicals only when necessary. Try to limit excessive pesticide usage and incorporate management strategies into a program along with chemical applications

APPENDIX A

The Basics—
Soil, Water and Grass

RULES OF THUMB FOR WATER USE ON LAWNS AND GARDENS
Courtesy of the United States Department of Agriculture (USDA)

One deep watering is much better than watering several times lightly.

Lawns need about one inch of water each week. If the weather is very hot, apply an inch of water about every three days.

Watering to a depth of four to six inches encourages deeper, healthier root development. It allows longer periods between watering.

To measure the water, put an empty tuna can (or cat food can) on the lawn while watering. Stop watering when the can is full or if you notice water running off the lawn.

KNOW YOUR SOIL

Different soil types have different watering needs. You don't need to be a soil scientist to know how to water your soil properly. These tips can help.

Loosen the soil around plants so it can quickly absorb water and nutrients.

Use a one- to two-inch protective layer of mulch on the soil surface above the root area. Cultivating and mulching reduce evaporation and soil erosion.

Clay soil: Add organic material such as compost or peat moss. Till or spade to help loosen the soil. Since clay soil absorbs water very slowly, water only as fast as the soil absorbs the water.

Sandy soil: Add organic material to supplement sandy soil. Otherwise, the water can run through it so quickly that plants won't be able to absorb it.

Loam soil: The best kind of soil. It's a combination of sand, silt, and clay. Loam absorbs water readily and stores it for plants to use.

WATER AT THE RIGHT TIME OF THE DAY

Early morning or night is the best time for watering to reduce evaporation.

To help control where your water goes, water when it's not windy.

RULES OF THUMB FOR PROPER FERTILIZER USE

Fertilizers provide nutrients necessary for plant health and growth, such as nitrogen, phosphorus, and potassium. These are what N, P, and K stand for on bags of fertilizer. Nitrogen (N) is needed for healthy green growth and regulation of other nutrients. Phosphorus (P) helps proper roots and seeds develop and resist disease. Potassium (K) is also important in root development and disease resistance. When properly applied, the nutrients in fertilizers are absorbed by plants and little of these nutrients enter ground or surface water resources.

Use the Right Fertilizer

Test your soil to find out what nutrients are needed. Contact your local Natural Resources Conservation Service or Cooperative State

Research, Education, and Extension Service office to get information on obtaining a soil test. Local fertilizer dealers can also be helpful.

A soil test will help you understand what your plants require. Follow label directions.

Choose a fertilizer that has at least one-fourth of the nitrogen in a slow-release form, such as sulphur-coated urea.

MOW YOUR LAWN FREQUENTLY

Leave the grass clippings to decompose on the lawn. Annually, this will provide nutrients equivalent to one or two fertilizer applications. Set mower at two inches to reduce water use during hot weather.

APPLY FERTILIZER PROPERLY

It is best to apply fertilizer when the soil is moist and then water lightly. This will help the fertilizer move into the root zone where it is available to the plants, rather than stay on top of the soil where it can be blown or washed away.

Watch the weather. Avoid applying it immediately before a heavy rain system is predicted to arrive. Too much rain (or sprinkler water) will take the nutrients away from the lawn's root zone.

Use the minimal amount of fertilizer necessary and apply it in small, frequent applications. An application of two pounds of fertilizer five times per year is better than five pounds of fertilizer twice a year.

Calibrate your fertilizer spreader to be sure you know exactly how much material is being discharged in a given space. Follow instructions accompanying your spreader.

When spreading fertilizer, cover ends of the lawn first, ten go back and forth across the rest of the lawn, using half of the recommended amount. Shut the spreader off before reaching the ends to avoid over-application. Apply the other half of the fertilizer going back and forth perpendicular to the first pattern.

Dispose of fertilizer bags or containers in a safe and state-approved manner.

ALTERNATIVES TO PESTICIDES AND CHEMICALS

When used incorrectly, pesticides can pollute water. They also kill beneficial as well as harmful insects. Natural alternatives prevent both of these events from occurring and save you money. Consider using natural alternatives for chemical pesticides: Non-detergent insecticidal soaps, garlic, hot pepper sprays, 1 teaspoon of liquid soap in a gallon of water, used dishwater, or forceful stream of water to dislodge insects.

Also consider using plants that naturally repel insects. These plants have their own chemical defense systems, and when planted among flowers and vegetables, they help keep unwanted insects away.

TURFGRASS QUESTIONS AND ANSWERS
Courtesy of the United States Department of Agriculture (USDA)

1) WHAT IS THE BEST SPECIES OF GRASS TO GROW WHERE I LIVE?

The turfgrasses are divided into cool-season and warm-season species.

Cool-season species do better in the cooler times of the year and thrive in temperatures from 65° to 75° F. Warm-season grasses are best adapted to temperatures between 80° and 95° F. The cool-season grasses grow well in the cooler regions of the northern United States and the warm-season species are best adapted to the warmer regions of the southern U.S. Grass species adaptation in the U.S., however, is a little more complicated than that, with the U.S. having four separate climatic zones of grass adaptation.

The cool humid zone encompasses the Northeast, several states of the Midwest, and much of the Pacific Northwest. The cool arid zone includes much of the dryer areas of the Midwest and West. Cool season species such as Bluegrass, fescues, ryegrasses, and bentgrasses are best adapted to the cool humid zone; however, Buffalograss and zoysiagrass, both warm season grasses, are found in the western and southern parts of this region even though the growing season is short for these species. The cool arid zone is basically a cool-season zone and any of the cool-season grasses can be used here if irrigation is available. Buffalograss is becoming widely used in the warmer parts of the region, such as Kansas, Nebraska, and Colorado, on non-irrigated sites. Less common cool-season species such as wheatgrasses and Canada bluegrass can be found on nonirrigated sites in the cooler parts of this zone.

Warm season species are best adapted to the warm arid and warm humid regions of the U.S. Bermudagrass is the most widely used species in the warm humid zone, although it is sometimes subject to winter damage in the northern parts of the zone. Zoysiagrass is widely used in the northern parts of this zone while carpetgrass, bahiagrass, and St. Augustinegrass are more common in the Gulf Coast region. Bermudagrass is also the most commonly used species in the warm arid zone, although any of the warm-season species can be used if irrigation is available. Buffalograss is becoming increasingly important in the more arid parts of this region. In both the warm arid and warm humid zones, cool-season species are often used for winter overseeding.

The U.S. also has a region known to the turf industry as the transition zone that extends through the central part of the country and includes parts of each of the other four zones. This is the most difficult region in which to grow grass. The transition zone is cold enough in the winter to make it difficult to maintain warm-season species and warm enough in the summer to make it difficult to grow cool-season species, therefore, no one species is well adapted in this region.

2) WHAT IS THE BEST CULTIVAR OF GRASS TO GROW WHERE I LIVE?

Turfgrass breeders throughout the U.S. have worked very hard to develop cultivars of the common turfgrass species that are well adapted to different regions of the country. In addition there is an excellent program, called the National Turfgrass Evaluation Program (NTEP), partially sponsored by the USDA that tests new and old standard cultivars of the most common turfgrass species at locations throughout the U.S. The results of these tests are available at the NTEP web site (www.ntep.org). Many of the evaluation sites are at public universities throughout the U.S., and university extension programs can generally provide data on the best locally adapted cultivars. In selecting an appropriate cultivar, it is generally best to select one that has rated high both locally and nationally, in other words, it rated within the top ten to twenty of the local test and its national average is in the top ten to twenty.

Once an acceptable cultivar has been selected, it is important to locate a source of high quality seed. Seed quality is one of the most often overlooked aspects of turfgrass establishment. If poor quality seed is selected, even the most intensive management efforts may not result in an acceptable turf.

Unfortunately many home and garden supply stores do not stock high quality seed, therefore, it can be difficult to locate the seed that you want. In some locations, agricultural seed supply stores may stock high quality seed of well-adapted cultivars. The Internet can also be searched to locate companies that deliver high quality seed by mail. The best way to determine if seed you are buying is high quality is to see if it has a state seed certification tag. The tag will indicate the level of germination of a selected sample and tell the relative percentage of important weeds and contaminating species.

3) THE BAG OF SEED I BOUGHT SAYS IT IS A MIXTURE OR A BLEND - WHAT DOES THAT MEAN?

A mixture is comprised of more than one species of grass. It is often advantageous to plant a mixture because of the increased range in genetic diversity and adaptive potential that is achieved. For example, in a lawn situation some areas may be shaded and others may receive full sun.

Additionally, some areas may have a droughty, course-textured sandy soil and others may have a fine-textured poorly drained clay. A mixture containing Kentucky bluegrass and red fescue contains species that can adapt and become dominant in these different environmental conditions. Red fescue will dominate in shaded areas and on infertile droughty soils, while Kentucky bluegrass will do well in full sunlight and on imperfectly drained, moist, fertile soils. The two species may also complement each other if one of the species is seriously damaged due to injury or disease.

A blend is when more than one cultivar within a species are blended together.

Blends can be useful in habitats where the environment is variable and a number of different disease and/or insect problems exist. Blends are valid where no one cultivar is resistant to all the major diseases within a habitat. If one cultivar is available that is resistant to all of the major disease and pest problems, then the use of a blend is not necessary.

4) WHAT ARE THE IMPORTANT THINGS TO CONSIDER WHEN ESTABLISHING A LAWN FROM SEED?

Successful establishment of a lawn from seed is a critical component of creating a healthy lawn; however, at times good establishment can even be difficult for professionals. The potential of successfully establishing a healthy turf can be increased by paying attention to a few basic principles.

Soil testing should be the first step in any soil preparation for turf establishment. A soil test should be done well in advance of planting to allow time for adding any soil amendments that may be needed. This is the best time to add fertilizer, lime, and other materials that may be needed. Rough grading of the existing soil or any new topsoil that was brought in is often necessary. In building construction, such as around new homes, where the top soil has been removed, 4 to 8 inches of topsoil should be placed on the site prior to establishment. Once the rough grading process has been completed, a starter fertilizer should be placed on the surface and not worked into the soil. A good choice for relatively fertile soils is a 12-25-10 fertilizer applied at a rate of 5 to 8 pounds of fertilizer per 1,000 ft². In the case of less fertile soils, where P (phosphorus) levels are relatively low, a material like 18-46-0 applied at the same rate may be more appropriate.

The time of seed application depends upon whether the grass is a cool-season or a warm-season species. Warm-season grasses established in temperate zones should be seeded in the spring as soon as soil temperatures are high enough to achieve germination. Cool-season grasses are best established in the late summer or early fall. It is important to apply the seed using the correct seeding rate.

The appropriate seeding rate is generally listed on the bag of seed. The grass seed is generally seeded on the surface and then lightly raked into the soil.

The smaller the seed, the shallower it should be planted. Very small seeds like creeping bentgrass will need to be very close to the surface, whereas larger seeds like tall fescue can emerge from depths of one half to one inch. The seed should also be spread as uniformly as possible by hand or using a mechanical spreader.

One of the keys to successful establishment is proper irrigation. The critical time is just after germination when the root system is not developed well enough to obtain sufficient moisture from the soil. Frequent irrigation is particularly important on warm windy days when the soil surface can dry out in a few hours.

The use of mulch such as straw can also help maintain adequate soil moisture during establishment.

5) HOW OFTEN SHOULD I FERTILIZE MY LAWN?

The general guideline for fertilizer application is to apply fertilizer when the turf is actively growing, therefore, the timing will be different for warm- and cool-season species. Cool-season species are most actively growing during the spring and fall of the year. However, high spring fertility treatments may be detrimental to the survival of the turf through the high stress periods of mid-summer. The general recommendation would be to apply 0.5 to 0.75 pound Nitrogen/1,000 ft^2 in March/April and May/June and one pound Nitrogen/1,000 ft^2 in August and September and again in the late fall. Total nitrogen applications to cool-season turf in temperate regions will generally range from three to five pounds N/1,000 ft^2 per year.

The general recommendation for warm-season turf species is 1 pound nitrogen/1,000 ft² per growing month. This is only a guideline. On heavier soils in drier conditions this will be too much. On sandy soils during periods of heavy rainfall, this will not be enough.

6) HOW SHORT CAN I MOW MY LAWN?

It is important to remember that turfgrasses do not thrive on mowing; they tolerate it. It may seem that mowing is good for the grass, but mowing is always a stress. The cutting of leaf tissue may allow disease organisms to enter the plant, and it reduces the photosynthetic area, lowering the production of carbohydrates that the plant needs to grow. Turfgrasses are the best-equipped plants on earth to tolerate this type of defoliation. If there were better-adapted species, they would be used in the place of grasses. The mowing height that a turf will tolerate is dependent on the species that are present.

The cool-season species primarily used in lawn situations are Kentucky bluegrass, tall fescue, and perennial ryegrass. These three species will do best at heights of one and one half to three inches, with higher mowing heights used during the high-temperature stress periods. Warm-season species such as Bermudagrass and Zoysiagrass can tolerate heights of one half inch or less, while Bahiagrass, carpetgrass, and centipedegrass do best at heights from one to three inches, and St. Augustinegrass should be mowed in the three to four inch range.

7) HOW OFTEN SHOULD I WATER MY LAWN?

This question does not have a simple answer because irrigation requirements vary with grass species, with soil type, and with environmental conditions. These factors often interact in complex ways that make decision making difficult. On average, turf will usually require from one to one and one hald inches of water per week for normal maintenance conditions. This can be provided by rainfall or irrigation or a combination of the two.

The best time to irrigate is another management decision that can impact turf quality. Overly wet conditions in the canopy can contribute to disease development. Nighttime watering will keep the turf wet for the longest period of time and should be avoided if possible. Watering during the day will allow the turf to dry quickly, but will increase water loss due to evaporation. All things considered, the early morning hours provide the best time for turf irrigation.

Water loss from evaporation will be less, and the turf will dry quickly in the morning.

8) HOW CAN I GROW GRASS UNDER MY TREES?

It can be very difficult to maintain a turf under shade conditions. However, a few management practices can improve the overall turf condition in these areas. Shade in home lawn situations is generally provided by trees, therefore, the pruning of limbs below 10 feet from the ground and selective pruning of limbs in the crown of the tree will allow more light to reach the turf and improve turf quality.

The choice of the correct turf species can also enhance the odds of a high quality shaded turf. Red fescue is the cool-season species with the best shade tolerance and tall fescue will also do well in the shade. St. Augustine grass is the warm-season species with the best shade tolerance, but zoysiagrass will also perform well under shaded conditions.

TABLE A-1
Shapes and size classes of soil structure.†

	Shape of structure					
	Units are flat and platelike. They are generally oriented horizontally and faces are mostly horizontal	Units are prismlike and bounded by flat to rounded vertical faces. Units are distinctly longer vertically than horizontally; vertices angular.		Units are blocklike or polyhedral with flat or slightly rounded surfaces that are casts of the faces of surrounding peds; nearly equidimensional		Units are approximately spherical or polyhedral and are bounded by curved or very irregular faces that are not casts of adjoining peds
		Tops of units are indistinct and normally flat.	Tops of units are very distinct and normally rounded.	Faces intersect at relatively sharp angles	Mixture of rounded and plane faces and the vertices are mostly rounded	
Size class	Platy	Prismatic	Columnar	Angular blocky	Subangular blocky	Granular
	mm	mm	mm	mm	mm	mm
Very fine or very thin‡	<1	<10	<10	<5	<5	<1
Fine or thin‡	1-2	10-20	10-20	5-10	5-10	1-2
Medium	2-5	20-50	20-50	10-20	10-20	2-5
Coarse or thick‡	5-10	50-100	50-100	20-50	20-50	5-10
Very coarse or very thick‡	>10	>100	>100	>50	>50	>10

† From: Soil survey division staff. 1993. *Soil survey manual*, USDA-SCS Agric. Handb. 18. U.S. Gov. Print. Office, Washington, DC.
‡ In describing plates, *thin* is used instead of *fine* and *thick* is used instead of *coarse*.

APPENDIX B

Construction Tips

HOME AND GARDEN TIPS–CONSTRUCTION
Courtesy of the United States Department of Agriculture (USDA)

NEW CONSTRUCTION

More often than not, soil will be without grass, trees, shrubs, and other plants at some time during construction. Without this protective vegetation, storms can move the soil into your neighbor's yard, clog storm drains and streams, and carry pesticides and nutrients into the water.

During Construction

Cover a bare area with mulch, such as straw, grass clippings, stones, wood chips, and other protective cover.

On steeper slopes, you should cover the mulch with burlap netting for extra protection. Vegetated and mulched areas increase water filtration into the soil, reducing erosive runoff water.

The key during and after construction is to control the concentrated flow of water. Watch where water runs off during storms. These are the areas of concentrated flow that need to be protected.

Act on what you learned by keeping grass in the channel on gentle slopes and lining the channel with stones or pavement on steep slopes.

After Construction

If the area you are building in has a steep slope, build terraces or steps made of logs or old railroad ties across the slope to divert water away from slopes and prevent soil erosion.

Between the steps, spread a thick layer of wood chips to protect the soil.

If the slope is gentle, seeding grass may be enough.

Use splash guards on gutter outlets to help reduce erosion at the foundation of your home.

Landscaping

Select plants that grow well in your area and are suitable for the climate conditions in your yard (sunny/shaded areas or wet/dry soil).

Plant ground covers, such as English Ivy and Asian Jasmine, in shaded areas where grass is difficult to establish and maintain.

Consult your local nursery for ground covers that grow well in your area. Ask about landscaping plants that mimic nature and consume little water.

Aesthetics

Plant windbreaks of trees or shrubs to reduce soil loss from blowing wind and also to provide habitat and shelter for wildlife. Windbreaks reduce the wind around your home and serve as a sight and sound barrier.

TERRACING
Courtesy of the United States Department of Agriculture (USDA)

Use terraces to make flower and vegetable gardening possible on steep slopes, or simply to add interest to your landscape.

IN YOUR BACKYARD

Terraces can create several mini-gardens in your backyard. On steep slopes, terracing can make planting a garden possible. Terraces prevent erosion by shortening the long slope into a series of shorter, more level steps. This allows heavy rains to soak into the soil rather than run off and cause erosion.

MATERIALS FOR TERRACES

Numerous materials are available for building terraces. Treated wood is often used because of several advantages: it is easy to work with, blends well with plants, and is often less expensive than other materials. There are many types of treated wood on the market–from railroad ties to landscaping timbers. These materials will last for years. While there has been some concern about using these treated materials around plants, studies by Texas A&M University and the Southwest Research Institute concluded that these materials are not harmful to gardens or people when used as recommended. Other materials for terraces include bricks, rocks, concrete blocks, and similar masonry materials. Some masonry materials are made specifically for walls and terraces and can be more easily installed by a homeowner than other materials such as field stone and brick. Most stone or masonry products tend to be more expensive than wood.

HEIGHT OF WALLS

The steepness of the slope often dictates wall height. Make the terraces in your yard high enough so the land between them is fairly level. Be sure the terrace material is strong enough and anchored well enough to stay in place through freezing and thawing, and heavy rainstorms.

Do not underestimate the pressure of water-logged soil behind a wall. It can be enormous and cause improperly constructed walls to bulge or collapse. Many communities have building codes for walls and terraces. Large projects will need the expertise of a professional to make sure the walls can stand up to water pressure in the soil. Large terraces also need to be built with proper drainage and to be tied back into the slope properly. Because of the expertise and equipment required to do this correctly, you will probably want to restrict terraces you build yourself to no more than a foot or two high.

BUILDING A TERRACE

The safest way to build a terrace is probably the cut-and-fill method. With this method little soil is disturbed, giving you protection from erosion should a sudden storm occur while the work is in progress. This method will also require little, if any, additional soil.

Contact your utility companies to identify the location of any buried utilities before starting to excavate.

Determine the rise and run of your slope. The rise is the vertical distance from the bottom of the slope to the top. The run is the horizontal distance between the top and bottom. This will help you determine how many terraces you need. For example, if your run is 20 feet and the rise is eight feet and you want each bed to be five feet wide, you will need four beds. The rise of each bed will be two feet.

Start building beds at the bottom of your slope. You will need to dig a trench in which to place your first tier. The depth and width of the trench will vary depending on how tall the terrace will be and the specific building materials you are using. Follow the manufacturer's instructions carefully when using masonry products. Many of these have limits to the number of tiers or the height that can be safely built. If using landscape timbers and your terrace is low (less than 2 feet), you only need to bury the timber to about half its thickness or less. The width of the trench should be slightly wider than your timber. Make sure the bottom of the trench is firmly packed and completely level. Place your timbers in the trench.

For the sides of your terrace, dig a trench into the slope. The bottom of this trench must be level with the bottom of the first trench. When the depth of the trench is one inch greater than the thickness of your timber, you have reached the back of the terrace and can stop digging.

Cut a timber to the correct length and place in trench.

Drill holes through your timbers and pound long spikes or pipes through the holes and into the ground. A minimum of 18 inches pipe length is recommended; longer pipes may be needed for stability for higher terraces.

Place the next tier of timbers on top of the first, overlapping corners and joints. Spike these together.

Move soil from the back of the bed to the front of the bed until the surface is level. Add another tier as needed.

Repeat, starting with step 2. In continuously connected terrace systems, the first timber of the second tier will also be the back wall of your first terrace.

The back wall of the last bed will be level with the front wall of that bed.

When finished, plant and mulch.

OTHER OPTIONS FOR SLOPES

If terraces are beyond the limits of your time or money, you may want to consider other options for backyard slopes. If you have a slope that is hard to mow, consider using groundcovers other than grass. There are many plants adapted to a wide range of light and moisture conditions that require little care, but provide soil erosion protection. These include:

- Juniper (Juniperus horizontalis)
- Pachysandra (Pachysandra terminalis)
- Wintercreeper (Euonymus fortunei)
- Periwinkle (Vinca minor)

- Cotoneaster (Cotoneaster spp.)
- Potentilla (Potentilla spp.)
- Partridge berry (Gaultheria procumbens)
- Heathers and heaths

Strip-cropping is another way to deal with long slopes. Rather than terracing to make garden beds level, plant perennial beds and strips of grass across the slope. Once established, many perennials are effective in reducing erosion. Mulch also helps reduce erosion. The erosion that may occur will be primarily limited to the garden area. The grass strips will act as filter strips and catch much of the soil that may run off the beds. Grass strips should be wide enough to mow across the hill easily as well as wide enough to effectively reduce erosion.

ON THE FARM

Terraces catch runoff water, let the water soak into the ground, and deliver the excess safely to the bottom of a hillside much like eave spouts on a house. The earthen ridges built around a hillside on the contour cut a long slope into shorter slopes, preventing water from building to a highly erosive force. Some terraces are seeded to grass, which provides erosion control and a nesting area for birds. Terraces are often used in combination with other conservation practices to provide more complete soil protection.

Strip-cropping is a common erosion control practice on many farms. Farmers often alternate strips of corn or soybeans with strips of hay. Many farmers put erosion-prone areas into permanent cover.

APPENDIX C

Compost and Mulch Tips

COMPOSTING
Courtesy of the United States Department of Agriculture (USDA)

Compost is a dark, crumbly mixture of decomposed organic matter, such as grass clippings, leaves, twigs, and branches.

HOW DOES COMPOSTING WORK?

Even the first-time composter can make good quality compost. Like good cooking, composting is part science, part art. Attention to the following parameters will help you get started.

MATERIALS

Anything that was once alive will naturally decompose. However, some organic wastes should not be composted at home.

DO compost these items: grass clippings, leaves, plant stalks, hedge trimmings, old potting soil, twigs, annual weeds without seed heads, vegetable scraps, coffee filters, and tea bags.

Do NOT compost these items: diseased plants, weeds with seed heads, invasive weeds such a quack grass and morning glory, pet feces, dead animals, bread and grains, meat or fish parts, dairy products, grease, cooking oil, or oily foods.

MAKING IT WORK

To prepare compost, organic material, microorganisms, air, water, and a small amount of nitrogen are needed.

Organic material is leaves, grass clippings, etc. that you are trying to decompose. Microorganisms are small forms of plant and animal life, which break down the organic material. A small amount of garden soil or manure provides sufficient microorganisms.

The nitrogen, air, and water provide a favorable environment for the microorganisms to make the compost. A small amount of nitrogen fertilizer can add sufficient nitrogen to the compost. You can purchase nitrogen fertilizers at many hardware stores, feed stores, or nurseries.

Air is the only part which cannot be added in excess. Too much nitrogen can kill microbes; too much water causes insufficient air in the pile.

BIOLOGY

Bacteria are the first to break down plant tissue and are the most numerous and effective compost makers in your compost pile. Fungi and protozoa soon join the bacteria and, somewhat later in the cycle, centipedes, millipedes, beetles, and worms complete the composting process.

SURFACE AREA

If the microorganisms have more surface area to feed on, the materials will break down faster. Chopping your garden debris with a machete, or using a chipper, shredder, or lawnmower to shred materials will help them decompose faster.

VOLUME

Compost piles trap heat generated by the activity of millions of microorganisms. A 3-foot by 3-foot by 3-foot compost pile is considered a minimum size for hot, fast composting. Piles wider or taller than 5 feet don't allow enough air to reach the microorganisms at the center.

MOISTURE AND AERATION

The microorganisms in the compost pile function best when the materials are as damp as a wrung-out sponge and have many air passages. Extremes of sun or rain can adversely affect the balance of air and moisture in your pile. The air in the pile is usually used up faster than the moisture, so the materials must be turned or mixed up occasionally to add air that will sustain high temperatures and control odor. Materials can be turned with a pitchfork, rake, or other garden tool.

TIME AND TEMPERATURE

The most efficient decomposing bacteria thrive in temperatures between 110°F and 160°F. Thus, the hotter the pile, the faster the composting. If you achieve a good balance of carbon and nitrogen, provide lots of surface area within a large volume of material, and maintain adequate moisture and aeration, the temperature will rise over several days.

USES FOR COMPOST

Compost contains nutrients, but it is not a substitute for fertilizers. Compost holds nutrients in the soil until plants can use them, loosens and aerates clay soils, and retains water in sandy soils.

To use as a soil amendment, mix 2 to 5 inches of compost into vegetable and flower gardens each year before planting.

In a potting mixture, add one part compost to two parts commercial potting soil, or make your own mixture by using equal parts of compost and sand or perlite.

As a mulch, spread an inch or two of compost around annual flowers and vegetables, and up to 6 inches around trees and shrubs.

As a top dressing, mix finely sifted compost with sand and sprinkle evenly over lawns.

MULCHING TIP SHEET
Courtesy of the United States Department of Agriculture (USDA)

Mulching enriches and protects soil, helping provide a better growing environment.

IN YOUR BACKYARD

Mulching is one of the simplest and most beneficial practices you can use in the garden. Mulch is simply a protective layer of a material that is spread on top of the soil. Mulches can either be organic–such as grass clippings, straw, bark chips, and similar materials–or inorganic–such as stones, brick chips, and plastic. Both organic and inorganic mulches have numerous benefits.

Mulch:

- Protects the soil from erosion
- Reduces compaction from the impact of heavy rains
- Conserves moisture, reducing the need for frequent waterings
- Maintains a more even soil temperature
- Prevents weed growth
- Keeps fruits and vegetables clean
- Keeps feet clean, allowing access to garden even when damp
- Provides a "finished" look to the garden

Organic mulches also improve the condition of the soil. As these mulches slowly decompose, they provide organic matter which helps keep the soil loose. This improves root growth, increases the infiltration of water, and also improves the water-holding capacity of the soil. Organic matter is a source of plant nutrients and provides an ideal environment for earthworms and other beneficial soil organisms.

While inorganic mulches have their place in certain landscapes, they lack the soil improving properties of organic mulches. Inorganic mulches, because of their permanence, may be difficult to remove if you decide to change your garden plans at a later date. Therefore, this tip sheet is limited to the use of organic mulches.

MULCH MATERIALS

You can find mulch materials in your own yard! Lawn clippings make excellent mulch. While not particularly attractive for a flower bed, they work wonderfully in the vegetable garden. The fine texture allows them to be spread easily even around small plants. However, grass clippings are becoming scarce because of the increased popularity of mulching lawnmowers that provide many of the same benefits of mulching to lawns. Newspaper, as a mulch, works especially well to control weeds. Leaves are another readily available material to use as mulch. Leaf mold, or the decomposed remains of leaves, gives the forest floor its absorbent spongy structure. Compost makes a wonderful mulch if you have a large supply. Compost not only improves the soil structure but provides an excellent source of plant nutrients.

Bark chips and composted bark mulch are available at garden centers. These make a neat finish to the garden bed and will eventually improve the condition of the soil. These may last for one to three years or more depending on the size of the chips or how well composed the bark mulch is. Smaller chips tend to be easier to spread, especially around small plants. Depending on where you live, numerous other materials make excellent mulches. Hay and straw work well in the vegetable garden, although they may harbor weed seeds. Seaweed mulch, ground corn cobs, and pine needles can also be used. Pine needles tend to increase the acidity of the soil so they work best around acid-loving plants such as rhododendrons and blueberries.

WHEN TO APPLY MULCH

Time of application depends on what you hope to achieve by mulching. Mulches, by providing an insulating barrier between the soil and the air, moderate the soil temperature. This means that a mulched soil in the summer will be cooler than an adjacent unmulched soil; while in the winter, the mulched soil may not freeze as deeply. However, since mulch acts as an insulating layer, mulched soils tend to warm up more slowly in the spring and cool down more slowly in the fall than unmulched soils.

If you are using mulches in your vegetable garden or flower garden, it is best to apply them after the soil has warmed up in the spring. Cool, wet soils tend to slow seed germination and increase the decay of seeds and seedlings.

If adding additional layers of mulch to existing perennial beds, wait until the soil has warmed completely.

Mulches used to help moderate winter temperatures can be applied late in the fall after the ground has frozen but before the coldest temperatures arrive. Applying mulches before the ground has frozen may attract rodents looking for a warm over-wintering site. Delayed applications of mulch should prevent this problem as, hopefully, the creatures would already have found some other place to nest!

Mulches used to protect plants over winter should be loose material such as straw, hay, or pine boughs that will help insulate the plants without compacting under the weight of snow and ice. One of the benefits from winter applications of mulch is the reduction in the freezing and thawing of the soil in the late winter and early spring. These repeated cycles of freezing at night and then thawing in the warmth of the sun cause many small or shallow rooted plants to be heaved out of the soil. This leaves their root systems exposed and results in injury or death. Mulching helps prevent the rapid fluctuations in soil temperature and reduces the chances of heaving.

APPLYING MULCH

Begin by asking yourself the following questions:

- What do I hope to achieve by mulching?
- Weed control?
- Moisture retention?
- Soil improvement?
- Beautification?
- How large is the area to be mulched?
- How much mulch will I need to cover the area?

Mulch is measured in cubic feet. As an example, if you have an area 10 feet by 10 feet and you wish to apply three inches of mulch, you would need 25 cubic feet.

Determine what mulch material to use and purchase or accumulate what you need.

Mulch can often be purchased bagged or bulk from garden centers. Bulk may be cheaper if you need large volumes and have a way to haul it. Bagged mulch is often easier to handle, especially for smaller projects. Most bagged mulch comes in three-cubic-feet bags.

COMPOST

Refer to the tip sheet on composting for information on how to make your own compost.

LEAVES

Collect leaves in the fall.

Chop with a lawnmower or shredder. Whole leaves tend to compact if wet or blow away if dry. Chopping will reduce the volume and facilitate composting.

Compost leaves over winter. Some studies have indicated that freshly chopped leaves may inhibit the growth of certain crops. Therefore, it may be advisable to compost the leaves over winter before spreading them.

GRASS CLIPPINGS

Spread them immediately to avoid heating and rotting.

NEWSPAPER

Save your own newspapers.

Only use newspaper text pages (black ink); color dyes may be harmful to soil microflora and fauna if composted and used.

Use three or four sheets together, anchored with grass clippings or other mulch material to prevent blowing away.

The amount of mulch to apply will be determined by the mulch material you are using.

GENERAL GUIDELINES

Do not apply mulch directly in contact with plants. Leave an inch or so of space next to plants to help prevent diseases flourishing from excessive humidity.

Remove weeds before spreading mulch.

Bark mulch and wood chips are sometimes used with landscape fabric or plastic. The fabric or plastic is laid on top of the soil and then covered with a layer of bark chips. A caution to this practice: while initially the plastic or fabric may provide additional protection against weeds, as the mulch breaks down, weeds will start to grow in the mulch itself. The barrier between the soil and the mulch also prevents any improvement in the soil condition and makes planting additional plants more difficult.

FOR SOURCES OF MULCH

Check under mulches or garden centers or nurseries in the Yellow Pages. Your community may also have wood chips from the removal of street trees that are available free to residents.

ON THE FARM

Farmers use mulches in many ways. Conservation tillage is a common practice that creates a mulch on the soil surface. Unlike the once common practice of plowing all crop residue into the soil, conservation tillage leaves the crop residue on top of the soil. These pieces of corn stalk, straw, or bean stems help protect the soil against wind and water erosion. Corn crops harvested for the grain return large amounts of residue to the soil surface and are more effective in preventing soil erosion than crops with less residue such as soybeans.

Mulching is a common practice among strawberry growers in northern climates. In this situation, mulch is used to protect the crop during the winter and to help prevent early blooming of the plants. Plants that bloom too early are more likely to be damaged by spring frosts. The mulch also helps keep the berries cleaner, protecting them from soil splashing on them in the rain.

Inorganic mulches are also widely used in commercial agriculture. Clear plastic mulch can be particularly beneficial in giving warm season crops a head start. The clear plastic acts as a mini-greenhouse, warming the soil underneath it. Particularly where early sweet corn brings a premium price, this practice can give a grower a couple of weeks head start.

Also, research is showing that leaving crop residues helps hold carbon in the soil and aids in reducing greenhouse gases.

MULCH MATERIALS

BARK MULCH

Apply two to four inches. Smaller chips are easier to spread, especially around small plants. Excellent for use around trees, shrubs, and perennial gardens. When spreading mulch around trees, keep the mulch an inch or two away from the trunk. A couple inches of mulch is adequate.

There is no need to apply the mulch 6 or 8 inches high, as often is seen.

WOOD CHIPS

Apply two to four inches. Similar to bark mulch. If using fresh wood chips that are mixed with a lot of leaves, composting may be beneficial.

LEAVES

Apply three to four inches. Best to chop and compost before spreading. If using dry leaves, apply about 6 inches.

GRASS CLIPPINGS

Apply two to three inches. Thicker layers tend to compact and rot, becoming quite slimy and smelly. Add additional layers as clippings decompose. Do not use clippings from lawns treated with herbicides.

NEWSPAPER

Apply ¼ inch. Apply sheets of newspaper and cover lightly with grass clippings or other mulch material to anchor. If other mulch materials are not available, cover edges of paper with soil. Applying on a windy day can be a problem.

COMPOST

Apply three to four inches. Excellent material for enriching soil.

APPENDIX D

Pests

THE LIVING SOIL: FUNGI

By Elaine R. Ingham
Courtesy of the United States Department of Agriculture (USDA)

Fungi are microscopic cells that usually grow as long threads or strands called hyphae, which push their way between soil particles, roots, and rocks. Hyphae are usually only several thousandths of an inch (a few micrometers) in diameter. A single hyphae can span in length from a few cells to many yards. A few fungi, such as yeast, are single cells.

Hyphae sometimes group into masses called mycelium or thick, cord-like "rhizomorphs" that look like roots. Fungal fruiting structures (mushrooms) are made of hyphal strands, spores, and some special structures like gills on which spores form. (See figure) A single individual fungus can include many fruiting bodies scattered across an area as large as a baseball diamond.

Fungi perform important services related to water dynamics, nutrient cycling, and disease suppression. Along with bacteria, fungi are important as decomposers in the soil food web. They convert hard-to-digest organic material into forms that other organisms can use. Fungal hyphae physically bind soil particles together, creating stable aggregates that help increase water infiltration and soil water holding capacity.

Soil fungi can be grouped into three general functional groups based on how they get their energy. Decomposers - saprophytic fungi - convert dead organic material into fungal biomass, carbon dioxide (CO_2), and small molecules, such as organic acids. These fungi generally use complex substrates, such as the cellulose and lignin, in wood, and are essential in decomposing the carbon ring structures in some pollutants. A few fungi are called "sugar fungi" because they use the same simple substrates as do many bacteria. Like bacteria, fungi are important for immobilizing, or retaining, nutrients in the soil. In addition, many of the secondary metabolites of fungi are organic acids, so they help increase the accumulation of humic-acid rich organic matter that is resistant to degradation and may stay in the soil for hundreds of years.

Mutualists—the mycorrhizal fungi—colonize plant roots. In exchange for carbon from the plant, mycorrhizal fungi help solubolize phosphorus and bring soil nutrients (phosphorus, nitrogen, micronutrients, and perhaps water) to the plant. One major group of mycorrhizae, the ectomycorrhizae, grow on the surface layers of the roots and are commonly associated with trees. The second major group of mycorrhizae are the endomycorrhizae that grow within the root cells and are commonly associated with grasses, row crops, vegetables, and shrubs. Arbuscular mycorrhizal (AM) fungi are a type of endomycorrhizal fungi. Ericoid mycorrhizal fungi can by either ecto- or endomycorrhizal.

The third group of fungi, pathogens or parasites, cause reduced production or death when they colonize roots and other organisms. Root-pathogenic fungi, such as Verticillium, Pythium, and Rhizoctonia, cause major economic losses in agriculture each year. Many fungi help control diseases. For example, nematode-trapping fungi that parasitize disease-causing nematodes, and fungi that feed on insects may be useful as biocontrol agents.

WHERE ARE FUNGI?

Saprophytic fungi are commonly active around woody plant residue. Fungal hyphae have advantages over bacteria in some soil environments. Under dry conditions, fungi can bridge gaps between pockets of moisture and continue to survive and grow, even when soil moisture is too low for most bacteria to be active. Fungi are able to use nitrogen up from the soil, allowing them to decompose surface residue which is often low in nitrogen.

Fungi are aerobic organisms. Soil which becomes anaerobic for significant periods generally loses its fungal component. Anaerobic conditions often occur in waterlogged soil and in compacted soils.

Fungi are especially extensive in forested lands. Forests have been observed to increase in productivity as fungal biomass increases.

THE LIVING SOIL: PROTOZOA

By Elaine R. Ingham
Courtesy of the United States Department of Agriculture (USDA)

Protozoa are single-celled animals that feed primarily on bacteria, but also eat other protozoa, soluble organic matter, and sometimes fungi. They are several times larger than bacteria - ranging from $1/5{,}000$ to $1/50$ of an inch (5 to 500 µm) in diameter. As they eat bacteria, protozoa release excess nitrogen that can then be used by plants and other members of the food web.

Protozoa are classified into three groups based on their shape: Ciliates are the largest and move by means of hair-like cilia. They eat the other two types of protozoa, as well as bacteria. Amoebae also can be quite large and move by means of a temporary foot or "pseudopod." Amoebae are further divided into testate amoebae (which make a shell-like covering) and naked amoebae (without a covering). Flagellates are the smallest of the protozoa and use a few whip-like flagella to move.

WHAT DO PROTOZOA DO?

Protozoa play an important role in mineralizing nutrients, making them available for use by plants and other soil organisms. Protozoa (and nematodes) have a lower concentration of nitrogen in their cells than the bacteria they eat. (The ratio of carbon to nitrogen for protozoa is 10:1 or much more and 3:1 to 10:1 for bacteria.) Bacteria eaten by protozoa contain too much nitrogen for the amount of carbon protozoa need. They release the excess nitrogen in the form of ammonium (NH^{4+}). This usually occurs near the root system of a plant. Bacteria and other organisms rapidly take up most of the ammonium, but some is used by the plant. (See figure for explanation of mineralization and immobilzation.)

Another role that protozoa play is in regulating bacteria populations. When they graze on bacteria, protozoa stimulate growth of the bacterial population (and, in turn, decomposition rates and soil aggregation). Exactly why this happens is under some debate, but grazing can be thought of like pruning a tree - a small amount enhances growth, too much reduces growth or will modify the mix of species in the bacterial community.

Protozoa are also an important food source for other soil organisms and help to suppress disease by competing with or feeding on pathogens.

WHERE ARE PROTOZOA?

Protozoa need bacteria to eat and water in which to move, so moisture plays a big role in determining which types of protozoa will be present and active. Like bacteria, protozoa are particularly active in the rhizosphere next to roots.

Typical numbers of protozoa in soil vary widely—from a thousand per teaspoon in low fertility soils to a million per teaspoon in some highly fertile soils. Fungal-dominated soils (e.g. forests) tend to have more testate amoebae and ciliates than other types. In bacterial-dominated soils, flagellates and naked amoebae predominate. In general, high clay-content soils contain a higher number of smaller protozoa (flagellates and naked amoebae), while coarser textured soils contain more large flagellates, amoebae of both varieties, and ciliates.

NEMATODES AND PROTOZOA

Protozoa and bacterial-feeding nematodes compete for their common food resource: bacteria. Some soils have high numbers of either nematodes or protozoa, but not both. The significance of this difference to plants is not known. Both groups consume bacteria and release NH^{4+}.

BUG BIOGRAPHY: SOIL DWELLING VAMPIRES

Most protozoa eat bacteria, but one group of amoebae, the vampyrellids, eat fungi. The perfectly round holes drilled through the fungal cell wall, much like the purported puncture marks on the neck of a vampire's victim, are evidence of the presence of vampyrellid amoebae. The amoebae attach to the surface of fungal hyphae and generate enzymes that eat through the fungal cell wall. The amoeba then sucks dry or engulfs the cytoplasm inside the fungal cell before moving on to its next victim.

Vampyrellids attack many fungi including root pathogens, such as Gaeumannomyces graminis, shown in the photo. This fungus attacks wheat roots and causes take-all disease.

TABLE D-1
Pests and plant repellents.

Pest	Plant Repellent
Ant	mint, tansy, pennyroyal
Aphids	mint, garlic, chives, coriander, anise
Bean Leaf Beetle	potato, onion, turnip
Codling Moth	common oleander
Colorado Potato Bug	green beans, coriander, nasturtium
Cucumber Beetle	radish, tansy
Flea Beetle	garlic, onion, mint
Imported Cabbage Worm	mint, sage, rosemary, hyssop
Japanese Beetle	garlic, larkspur, tansy, rue, geranium
Leaf Hopper	geranium, petunia
Mexican Bean Beetle	potato, onion, garlic, radish, petunia, marigolds
Mice	onion
Root Knot Nematodes	French marigolds
Slugs	prostrate rosemary, wormwood
Spider Mites	onion, garlic, cloves, chives
Squash Bug	radish, marigolds, tansy, nasturtium
Stink Bug	radish
Thrips	marigolds
Tomato Hornworm	marigolds, sage, borage
Whitefly	marigolds, nasturtium

Index

Page numbers in italics refer to figures